JOHN WOO'S
Bullet in the Head

Hong Kong University Press thanks Xu Bing for writing the Press's name in his Square Word Calligraphy for the covers of its books. For further information see p. iv.

THE NEW HONG KONG CINEMA SERIES

The New Hong Kong Cinema came into existence under very special circumstances, during a period of social and political crisis resulting in a change of cultural paradigms. Such critical moments have produced the cinematic achievements of the early Soviet cinema, neorealism, the *nouvelle vague*, and the German cinema of the 1970s and, we can now say, the New Hong Kong Cinema. If this cinema grew increasingly intriguing in the 1980s, after the announcement of Hong Kong's return to China, it is largely because it had to confront a new cultural and political space that was both complex and hard to define, where the problems of colonialism were uncannily overlaid with those of globalism. Such uncanniness could not be caught through straight documentary or conventional history writing: it was left to the cinema to define it.

Has the creative period of the New Hong Kong Cinema now come to an end? However we answer the question, there is a need to evaluate the achievements of Hong Kong cinema. This series distinguishes itself from the other books on the subject by focusing in-depth on individual Hong Kong films, which together make the New Hong Kong Cinema.

Series General Editors
Ackbar Abbas, Wimal Dissanayake, Mette Hjort, Gina Marchetti, Stephen Teo

Series Advisors
Chris Berry, Nick Browne, Ann Hui, Leo Lee, Li Cheuk-to, Patricia Mellencamp, Meaghan Morris, Paul Willemen, Peter Wollen, Wu Hung

Other titles in the series
Andrew Lau and Alan Mak's *Infernal Affairs – The Trilogy* by Gina Marchetti
Fruit Chan's *Durian Durian* by Wendy Gan
John Woo's *A Better Tomorrow* by Karen Fang
John Woo's *The Killer* by Kenneth E. Hall
Johnnie To Kei-fung's *PTU* by Michael Ingham
King Hu's *A Touch of Zen* by Stephen Teo
Mabel Cheung Yuen-ting's *An Autumn's Tale* by Stacilee Ford
Peter Ho-sun Chan's *He's a Woman, She's a Man* by Lisa Odham Stokes
Stanley Kwan's *Center Stage* by Mette Hjort
Tsui Hark's *Zu: Warriors From the Magic Mountain* by Andrew Schroeder
Wong Kar-wai's *Ashes of Time* by Wimal Dissanayake
Wong Kar-wai's *Happy Together* by Jeremy Tambling
Yuen Woo-ping's *Wing Chun* by Sasha Vojković

JOHN WOO'S
Bullet in the Head

Tony Williams

香 港 大 學 出 版 社
HONG KONG UNIVERSITY PRESS

Hong Kong University Press
14/F Hing Wai Centre
7 Tin Wan Praya Road
Aberdeen
Hong Kong

ISBN 978-962-209-968-5

British Library Cataloguing-in-Publication Data
A catalogue record for this book is available from the British Library.

Secure on-line Ordering
http://www.hkupress.org

Printed and bound by Condor Production Ltd., Hong Kong, China

Hong Kong University Press is honoured that Xu Bing, whose
art explores the complex themes of language across cultures,
has written the Press's name in his Square Word Calligraphy.
This signals our commitment to cross-cultural thinking and the
distinctive nature of our English-language books published in
China.

"At first glance, Square Word Calligraphy appears to be nothing
more unusual than Chinese characters, but in fact it is a new
way of rendering English words in the format of a square so they
resemble Chinese characters. Chinese viewers expect to be able
to read Square Word Calligraphy but cannot. Western viewers,
however are surprised to find they can read it. Delight erupts
when meaning is unexpectedly revealed."
— Britta Erickson, *The Art of Xu Bing*

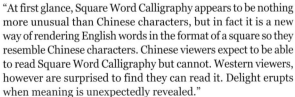

To John Woo and Waise Lee:
The Yin and Yang of *Bullet in the Head*
and
Sandie

Contents

Series Preface

The New Hong Kong Cinema came into existence under very special circumstances, during a period of social and political crisis resulting in a change of cultural paradigms. Such critical moments have produced the cinematic achievements of the early Soviet cinema, neorealism, the *nouvelle vague*, the German cinema in the 1970s and, we can now say, the recent Hong Kong cinema. If this cinema grew increasingly intriguing in the 1980s, after the announcement of Hong Kong's return to China, it was largely because it had to confront a new cultural and political space that was both complex and hard to define, where the problems of colonialism were overlaid with those of globalism in an uncanny way. Such uncanniness could not be caught through straight documentary or conventional history writing; it was left to the cinema to define it.

It does so by presenting to us an urban space that slips away if we try to grasp it too directly, a space that cinema coaxes into existence by whatever means at its disposal. Thus it is by eschewing a narrow idea of relevance and pursuing disreputable genres like melodrama, kung fu and the fantastic that cinema brings into view something else about the city which could otherwise be missed. One classic example is Stanley Kwan's *Rouge*, which draws on the unrealistic form of the ghost story to evoke something of the uncanniness of Hong Kong's urban space. It takes a ghost to catch a ghost.

In the New Hong Kong Cinema, then, it is neither the subject matter nor a particular set of generic conventions that is paramount. In fact, many Hong Kong films begin by following generic conventions but proceed to transform them. Such transformation of genre is also the transformation of a sense of place where all the rules have quietly and deceptively changed. It is this shifting sense of place, often expressed negatively and indirectly — but in the best work always rendered precisely in (necessarily) innovative images — that is decisive for the New Hong Kong Cinema.

Has the creative period of the New Hong Kong Cinema come to an end? However we answer the question, there is a need now to evaluate the achievements of Hong Kong cinema. During the last few years, a number of full-length books have appeared, testifying to the topicality of the subject. These books survey the field with varying degrees of success, but there is yet an almost complete lack of authoritative texts focusing in depth on individual Hong Kong films. This book series on the New Hong Kong Cinema is designed to fill this lack. Each volume will be written by a scholar/ critic who will analyse each chosen film in detail and provide a critical apparatus for further discussion including filmography and bibliography.

Our objective is to produce a set of interactional and provocative readings that would make a self-aware intervention into modern Hong Kong culture. We advocate no one theoretical position; the authors will approach their chosen films from their own distinct points of vantage and interest. The aim of the series is to generate open-ended discussions of the selected films, employing diverse analytical strategies, in order to urge the readers towards self-reflective engagements with the films in particular and the Hong Kong cultural space in general. It is our hope that this series will contribute to the sharpening of Hong Kong culture's conceptions of itself.

In keeping with our conviction that film is not a self-enclosed signification system but an important cultural practice among similar others, we wish to explore how films both reflect and inflect culture. And it is useful to keep in mind that reflection of reality and reality of reflection are equally important in the understanding of cinema.

Ackbar Abbas
Wimal Dissanayake

Acknowledgements

I wish to thank the following people who have been instrumental in helping me with this project. First, and foremost, I wish to thank Professor Gina Marchetti who suggested that I write this contribution to the Hong Kong University Press monograph series; Dr. Lisa Odham Stokes for the valuable material she has generously shared with me over the years; *Asian Cult Cinema* editor Tom Weisser who first introduced me to the area of Hong Kong cinema over fifteen years ago and has continued to stimulate me into exploring further rich domains of Southeast Asian film; Professor Ken Hall, author of the definitive work on John Woo, who has constantly inspired me with his frequent email correspondence and discussion of the director's work. John Charles was very generous in answering several enquiries and supplying me with a copy of the VCD version of the film which concluded with the alternative ending. Ryan Netzley offered expert assistance with his knowledge of Milton and apocalyptic interpretation. My one regret involves my inability to interview John Woo and Terence Chang who were in Mainland China making *Red Cliff* during the time I was writing this study. However, the appearance of another John Woo film is more important, especially if it reveals further evidence of a creative talent deserving more space for expression than the limiting confines of contemporary Hollywood action films. Last, but not least, I owe a lot to the helpful suggestions made by Colin Day, Michael Duckworth, and the anonymous reviewers of this work.

> "There's a long tradition of blood-thirsty drama going back to the Jacobeans, but without the poetry I think it's a bit cheap."[1]

1

The Apocalyptic Moment of
Bullet in the Head

Like many Hong Kong films of the 1980s and 90s, John Woo's *Bullet in the Head* contains grim forebodings then held by the former colony concerning its return to Mainland China in 1997. Despite the break from Maoism following the fall of the Gang of Four and Deng Xiaoping's movement towards capitalist modernization, the brutal events of Tiananmen Square caused great concern for a territory facing many changes in the near future. Even before these disturbing events Hong Kong's imminent return to a motherland with a different dialect and social customs evoked insecurity on the part of a population still remembering the violent events of the Cultural Revolution as well as the Maoist-inspired riots that affected the colony in 1967. Would the People's Liberation Army return to its former role by brutally punishing capitalist transgressors? Could Hong Kong witness its own version of Tiananmen Square if there were any democratic protests against the power of a Beijing-imposed chief executive? Residents would remember how Chairman Mao reversed his dictum of allowing "a thousand flowers to bloom" during the late 1950s. Johnny Mak's *The Long Arm of the Law* (1984–1989) "Big Circle" series of gangster films also depicted fear of lawless elements from the Mainland (often former members of the People's Liberation Army) committing acts of violence after crossing the border separating Guangzhou Province from Hong Kong.

Although Hong Kong cinema was not exclusively obsessed with 1997, fears concerning return to a motherland that many residents escaped from during the 1950s haunted several films. They could encompass an occasional reference to the necessity of learning Mandarin pronunciation as the clock began ticking towards 1997 in films such as Eddie Ma Poon-chiu's *Wicked City* (1992) as well as a grimmer vision like that contained in Tsui Hark's *We're Going to Eat You* (1980). Feelings about the implications of this "homecoming" occur in many Hong Kong films between 1984 and 1997. To ignore this current of thought or deny its contemporary influence does violence towards understanding important levels of meaning existing within these films. Social and historical contexts influence any work, whether artistic or popular. Although doomsday forecasts concerning Hong Kong's fate in 1997 proved fortunately to be in error, dark forebodings involving the colony's future were definitely present in many films before that date. Those critics who marginalize them in a different era of global capitalism do great disservice to understanding key implications contained within the material levels of a work. *Bullet in the Head* is a film containing references to 1997. But it also represents a last hurrah to those *yanggang* aspects of heroic bloodshed and male friendship seen in the films of Woo's mentor Zhang Che.[1] It is a much darker treatment of the Triad themes existing within *A Better Tomorrow* (1986) and *A Better Tomorrow 2* (1987) as well as the other concepts in Hong Kong's prolific gangster movie genre.

Woo gained important experience in his role as assistant director on two Zhang Che films, *The Boxer from Shantung* (1972) and *Blood Brothers* (1973) when he transferred to Shaw Brothers after working in Cathay Studios. He has frequently expressed his debt to Zhang Che and co-directed (with Wu Ma) a benefit film for his former mentor, *Just Heroes* (1989) that featured many of Zhang's actors as well as themes associated with him, particularly those important values of loyalty and friendship affected by a changing world. Woo develops many of Zhang Che's visual signatures, such as the use of slow-motion and close-ups, in creative and expressive ways. But he also continues to explore many of the violent *wuxia* themes of his mentor not just in his celebrated *A Better Tomorrow* films but also in his 1978 Golden Harvest film *Last Hurrah for Chivalry* as critics such as John Charles, Ken Hall, Michael Hoover, Lisa Odham Stokes, and Stephen Teo notice.[2]

The work of Zhang Che represents an apocalyptic current in Hong Kong cinema relevant to its own historical era. Reacting against what he felt were pale representations of males in earlier Hong Kong cinema, Zhang Che depicted his own version of heroic masculinity in films noted for high levels of bloodshed. Zhang's Wang Yu vehicles such as *Tiger Boy* (1965), *The One-Armed Swordsman* (1967), *The Assassin* (1967), *Golden Swallow* (1968), *Return of the One-Armed Swordsman* (1969), and those featuring Ti Lung and David Chiang such as *Vengeance* (1970), *The New One-Armed Swordsman* (1971), *Four Riders* (1971), *The Duel* (1971), *Duel of Fists* (1971), and *Blood Brothers* (1972), presented a world where traditional values of heroism, tradition, and knightly obligation became threatened by a changing era whether set in the distant or recent past. Influenced by a turbulent 1960s era characterized by social change, the Vietnam War, and the radical political experiments of Mao Zedong's Cultural Revolution, Zhang Che's "heroic bloodshed" films represented allegorical signifiers of a rapidly changing world heading towards an apocalyptic resolution anticipating the historical and political climax of Sam Peckinpah's *The Wild Bunch* (1969). The old world of noble heroes personified by the Confucian values of Kwan Tak-hing's Wong Feihung in the Cantonese cinema of the 1950s and early 1960s rapidly disappeared. Zhang Che's films revealed apocalyptic elements of grim forebodings. So did those later Hong Kong films made under the shadow of a feared return to China. The disastrous events of Tiananmen Square struck terror into the hearts and minds of Hong Kong citizens. At the same time, it must be said that a distinct difference existed between these films of Zhang Che and what John Woo would later attempt in *Bullet in the Head*. Zhang's type of apocalypse appeared to be more conservative in lamenting the loss of a masculinist world having little sympathy for the plight of women and the necessity for the development of a more positive context. Like Woo's film, the apocalypse took on bloody dimensions but a significant difference existed between the works of a director whose world appears to be regressively conservative and those films of his disciple that were more positive and politically nuanced in nature. This difference should alert us to the fact that the idea of apocalypse is more fluid and variable in nature than most conventional definitions suppose.

Most people understand apocalypse as a catastrophic climax for any world order. But an apocalyptic dimension may be symbolic as well as literal, having its own type of distinct cultural discursive connotation far more significant than any particular literal interpretation denoting the end of things. Despite the fact that any eschatological climax often does not occur in the lifetimes of those who expect the worse, this does rule out discarding the entire notion as a key element of meaning. Understanding what an apocalyptic feeling may have meant at a certain time within a definite historical era is always important.

Although the Early Church expected the imminent return of the Messiah within the lives of those he influenced on earth, later interpretations took on symbolic rather than literal dimensions. The chaotic nature of the return always receives emphasis. But each generation has its own cultural and symbolic interpretations of apocalypse influenced by contemporary historical events. Apocalypse generally refers to a literary corpus dealing with fears and expectations concerning the imminent arrival of the "last days" of human history. Associated with religious texts such as the Book of Revelations and other works contained in *The Apocrypha and Pseudepigrapha of the Old Testament*, the classical mode of this developing genre involves feelings of crisis and chaos associated with the culmination of human history, divine judgment, and the return of a Messianic figure who will herald the last days. Milton scholar Leland Ryken defines the concept as follows:

> The word "apocalypse" is derived from the Greek word meaning "to reveal." Accordingly, it has traditionally been used to describe writing which purports to be a revelation of phenomena which transcend the world of everyday reality. Apocalyptic writing has usually denoted prophetic writing — writing which is predicative of future events. Within this broad framework there are two main types of apocalyptic writing. One is concerned with a transcendental state, outside of time, which will follow history; such writing is eschatological orientated. The other views the apocalyptic state as attainable on earth, and describes a future state that will occur within the order of nature and within the ordinary temporal succession. Apocalypses of this type are frequently social in emphasis, with the reformed social order which is envisioned constituting a warning to contemporary society. Whether the future state is considered as falling within or beyond time, it is viewed as an ideal state — a type of golden age in which there is an ultimate triumph of good over evil.[3]

Social definitions of the apocalypse vary over historical eras. Ryken defines his version of the apocalypse as a transcendental state "placed either above or prior to ordinary time."[4] But the idea of the apocalypse in Hong Kong cinema is material in nature and highly pessimistic. It does envisage some form of cataclysmic "eschaton" though it has no defined concept of eschatology as opposed to religious interpretations. Warnings of what might happen certainly occur. But they comprise no sense of any idyllic future state nor any envisaged reformed social order but rather a different world which *may* differ radically from its former incarnation and involve elements of crisis, instability, and dislocation.[5] Apocalyptic literature also shares another common element with its modern counterparts. It is dualistic in nature, involving contrasting interpretations of conflicts between good and evil.[6] This parallels several features in *Bullet in the Head* involving contrasts between the honorable Frank and Vietnam Buddhist monks with the more evil figures of Paul and Mr. Leong as well as North and South Vietnamese opponents who share a common tendency towards violence transcending their oppositional political ideologies.

Even if the expected event does not occur within the period originally forecast, this does not invalidate investigating the nature of contemporary interpretations delivered within a certain social context. Although the "last days" did not occur within the lifetimes of the twelve disciples and the original members of the Early Church, the concept still remained and became subjected to various reinterpretations as it did in Milton's era. Ken Simpson notes this situation in terms of the changed perspectives undergone by John Milton in terms of their relationship to the different historical eras within which he worked.

> Whereas in 1641 Christ's return seemed imminent, in the decade after the Restoration the continuing spiritual struggle with Antichrist is emphasized. The turn to inwardness in the last stage of Milton's apocalyptic thought should not be confused with passivity, quietism, or indifference about the apocalypse, however. Vigorous spiritual preparedness is never absent from Milton's

early hope for a literal reign of Christ, but here it receives spiritual emphasis in the Restoration wilderness of persecution suffered by nonconformists, republicans, and the hero of *Paradise Regained.*[7]

Although certain critics deny historical and political factors affecting the contemporary Hong Kong films of John Woo and global cultural postmodernist scholars eagerly rejoice over the fact that those dark forebodings concerning 1997 never happened, this still does not invalidate the concept of an apocalyptic mood existing within a certain era of Hong Kong cinema as well as changes affecting its definition following the colony's return to the Mainland.[8] Precedents exist in previous eras as the above quotation reveals. Furthermore, no reputable Biblical or Milton scholar would reject earlier depictions of the Apocalypse in the Book of Revelations and allied texts on the grounds that since the events they described did not happen, these texts are irrelevant for understanding the mood of a particular era.

Unfortunately, a certain tendency exists in some areas of Hong Kong film scholarship to deny the importance of historical and material factors influencing the production of films made between 1984 and 1997 that involved fears concerning the return to the Mainland and what this might involve. Whether expressed in terms of apocalyptic bloodshed or minor plot motifs in films involving a character's desire to leave Hong Kong to begin a new career before the deadline of 1997 (as does Brigitte Lin's Jane Lin in the 1989 Film Workshop production *Web of Deception*), the historical moment of 1997 does occupy a major role in Hong Kong cinema of that time. Unfortunately, opposing arguments made by certain types of postmodernist scholars eager to deny the historical fears of that era represent a retrogressive opposing tendency. Others also attempt to deny the apocalyptic imminence of that moment by saying that as the dreaded event did not happen it is now therefore irrelevant in discussing that era of Hong Kong cinema. However, the arguments of local-based scholars such as Yau Ching, Stephen Teo, and Gina Marchetti and those outside such as David Bordwell, Lisa Odham Stokes, and Michael Hoover present an entirely different picture — to say nothing of John Woo some five years following 1997. The idea of apocalypse is diverse but relevant to understanding the context of *Bullet in the Head* as the following quotation shows.

If "Milton's great poems offer multiple, divergent, and indeed sometimes conflicting visions of the apocalypse and the millennium"— as another Milton scholar has remarked — the same is true both of *Bullet in the Head* and the different depictions of the apocalyptic moment in Hong Kong cinema.[9] In fact, the apocalypse may not have really gone away but changed its identity by accommodating itself to different circumstances.

Despite the fact that post-1997 Hong Kong is not the Restoration England of Charles II, it does have certain features in common in terms of contradictions and tensions existing within a particular social structure. Not everybody in England was happy with the Restoration of the Stuart Monarchy. Many cultural and political documents exist to reveal that this type of transition was not accepted by everyone, and certainly not by the Puritans! Hong Kong is still a territory exhibiting several tensions on political and artistic levels concerning its uneasy relationship with Mainland Chinese control under figures such as former Chief Executive Tung and his successors. As a specifically Hong Kong entity, the Hong Kong gangster film is currently indirectly dealing with political overtones as seen in the recent work of Johnnie To. He is now moving away from excessive exercises in style towards a more balanced cinema involving relevant material content as seen in *Election* (2005) and *Election 2* (2006).[10] To's recent films employ a significant socially conscious neo-noir style expressing feelings of insecurity and concern at the changing values of Hong Kong society nearly a decade after the restoration. Although To's neo-noir style does not reflect a "return of the repressed" politics directly paralleling those turbulent conditions of American postwar society (classical film noirs such as *Cornered* [1945] and *Crossfire* [1947] that appeared before the beginning of the blacklist period in late 1947), it does mediate apprehension concerning changing events following 1997. Despite not reflecting the apocalyptic tones of earlier pre-1997 films such as *Bullet in the Head*, To's two *Election* films depict the insecurity of a changing world in which the old values mean nothing as cynically demonstrated by the figure of Simon Yam Tat-wah's Lok who becomes displaced by Louis Koo's young successor seeking legitimacy. This new godfather instead finds himself trapped by a Mainland bureaucracy that will dominate his soul, the Triad community, and the colony in a far worse manner than anything ever envisaged by pre-1997 representations. The apocalypse arrives. But it is more in the nature of a "whimper" rather than a "bang." However, it is equally deadly as that depicted in John Woo's *Bullet in the Head*.

Made between his departure from Tsui Hark's Film Workshop and his final Golden Princess/Milestone production of *Hard Boiled* (1992), *Bullet in the Head*'s credits define it as the most auteur production of the director's career. Woo produced, directed, and co-scripted the work in very much the same manner as those early auteur-related films of Larry Cohen, Samuel Fuller, George Romero, and Tsui Hark himself, where the director occupies the key role in the cinematic process. The credits begin with the logo, "A John Woo Production" signifying a director now asserting his independence from Tsui Hark's producer function on the previous *A Better Tomorrow* films and *The Killer*. Woo worked on the screenplay with Patrick Leung Pak-yin and Janet Chun Siu-chun. *Bullet in the Head* represents one of his most personal works. Despite the type of misleading labels such as "master of violence" also applied to Sam Peckinpah, Woo's work actually transcends those reductive "blood and bullets" definitions mistakenly applied to his films by many who choose to confine him within generic brand labels and refuse to see other qualities inhabiting his work.

Bullet in the Head is a product of apocalyptic cinema. But at the same time it contains levels of meaning defying conventional definitions. The film combines two seemingly opposite concepts: apocalypse and melodrama, making *Bullet in the Head* more appropriately understood as an "apocalyptic melodrama." Western audiences usually associate melodrama with female-centered films dealing with domestic contradictions between home and independence according to classical representations associated with Hollywood cinema. But melodrama, especially in its Eastern representations, is more inclusive. It involves not only levels of masculine crisis seen occasionally in classical Hollywood examples such as *The Man from Laramie* (1955) and *Written on the Wind* (1956) but also other meanings extending far beyond domestic confines. Mainland Chinese and Hong Kong cinemas were acquainted with Hollywood melodrama and culturally inflected this genre in highly significant ways. As well as involving the female realm, melodramatic crisis could also encompass masculine issues, especially those having to do with cultural betrayal and challenges to traditional ways of living presented by new social codes. Cantonese and Mandarin branches of Hong Kong cinema contain many examples and they are not exclusively female-centered. Despite the violent nature of Zhang Che's films, they are often influenced by melodramatic issues as seen in *One Armed Swordsman, Return of the One Armed Swordsman, The Assassin*, and *Golden Swallow*. In *One Armed Swordsman*, Wang Yu's title hero becomes symbolically castrated by the daughter of a master who has adopted him. Although he accepts an alternative life by retreating to the country, he returns to defeat his master's adversary for the last time before retiring finally to his peaceful idyllic life of domesticity. The sequel sees him again reluctantly returning to his former defender role but now he becomes so disgusted by witnessing the betrayal of heroic values on the part of those he has defended that he retreats from the heroic world for the last time. In *The Assassin*, a contrast exists between the hero's desire for a peaceful union with his beloved and the bloody, heroic deed he has to perform at the climax in the name of duty. In *Golden Swallow*, Wang Yu's Silver Roc engages in masochistic death wish activities evoked by his dark desires for Cheng Pei-pei's title character. At the end of the film, Golden Swallow mourns Silver Roc. But unlike Wang Yu's one-armed swordsman, she cannot accept an alternative and peaceful life that Lo Lieh offers her.

These films operate on excessive levels and deal with conflicts between emotional desire and duty. Zhang Che's later films with Ti Lung and David Chiang further explore the melodramatic conflict between blood brotherhood and loyalty. In *Blood Brothers*, David Chiang's character avenges the betrayal of loyalty by Ti Lung who not only violates their close bonding but seduces the wife of Chen Kwan-tai and arranges his rival's death. This anticipates Paul's betrayal in *Bullet in the Head* although gold represents the motivation here rather than *Blood Brothers*'s sexual desire and social advancement. Ti Lung's character betrays friendship to secure his institutional advancement in the Ching dynasty establishment. Paul similarly succeeds Mr. Kwan/King in the Triad community in the final part of *Bullet in the Head* after betraying his other two friends and former blood brothers.

Betrayal is not taken lightly in these films since it violates codes of honor that operate as revered icons of respect in the worlds to which they belong. Those extreme representations involving bloodshed and violence in films that Western viewers often fail to comprehend actually depict an Eastern version of the "melodramatic excess" that appears in a different form within Hollywood melodrama. Many Western critics misunderstand personal dimensions in Woo's films, finding the presence of male emotional excess and violence foreign to their own experience. Homoerotic and/or sublimated gay overtone discourses dominate certain interpretations. However, *Bullet in the Head* is best understood as an apocalyptic melodrama. It unites opposing realms of the personal and the political within a narrative depicting a particular type of historical crisis casting former personal loyalties and traditional values into doubt. Excessive representations of masculine crisis may lead certain viewers to describe *Bullet in the Head* as "a tearjerker for men."[11] The film certainly contains such emotional qualities but these need to be understood within a certain cultural context. The use of music described by John Charles in his brief analysis actually serves to help viewers to understand more appropriately those important elements of melodramatic excess employed in this film. In earlier VHS copies of *Bullet in the Head*, the music functions as an overpowering element accompanying the descent of the gentle Frank into inhumane violent debasement. It forms a key punctuating aural device depicting an individual trapped into becoming an animal by overwhelming historical forces he has no control over.

Bullet in the Head is a film of personal and historical crisis. As well as being a great achievement of Hong Kong cinema, it is Woo's creative merger of two opposing symbolic modes of interpretation justifying a more appropriate understanding of *Bullet in the Head* as an "apocalyptic melodrama" rather than a spectacular action film. The apocalypse defines some world-threatening cataclysm in which things will never be the same again. Emphasis usually falls upon the historically spectacular definition of how the "last days" will occur. When the three friends arrive in Saigon, they witness events deliberately modeled on the 1989 Tiananmen Square incident. Vietnam functions as a "future perfect" representation of what *might* happen in 1997. It becomes a symbolic apocalypse characterized by bloodshed and violence. Another future "dispersion" symbolically appears in those later scenes showing Ben as a refugee among the Vietnamese seeking to escape the takeover of their country. The sequence evokes those earlier flights of Chinese citizens fleeing Mainland China after the victory of Mao's forces in 1949 as well as those escaping the violence of the Cultural Revolution a generation later.

By contrast, melodrama focuses upon personal dilemmas whether involving males or females. As Patrick Leung points out, the original Cantonese title *Dip huet gaai tau* (Mandarin, *Die xie jie tou*) literally translated as "Bloodshed on the streets," refers to the streets in terms of being the area of the lower classes during the late 1960s.[12] The film begins in the mean streets of the impoverished areas of Hong Kong and ends on the Ching Yu dock area of the colony. Since the first part of the film focuses upon the life of three lower-class male characters, an element that John Woo has described as "biographical," it is not surprising that the film contains melodramatic associations very much in the tradition of Cantonese social cinema such as Lung Gong's *Story of a Discharged Prisoner* (1967) and *Teddy Girls* (1969).[13] The wedding of Ben and Jane is a community event in the first part of the film since it is set in a long-vanished environment where poor people lived in council estates with courtyards facing each other and had daily contact unlike those contemporary isolated high-rise small apartments seen in films such as *Underground Banker* (1993). Although the 1950s Cantonese socially conscious world of *The House of 72 Tenants* (last filmed by Shaw Brothers in 1973) has now virtually disappeared, the proximity of people living close to each other and discovering their problems still exists as depicted in the wedding night scene of Ben seeing Frank being thrown out by his parents. Ben then decides to avenge Frank as a matter of honor. Contrast between the codes of friendship and loyalty shared between Ben and Frank and the more inhumane mercenary values influencing Paul form key melodramatic components in a film where personal issues are always paramount.

Bullet in the Head was designed to be entirely distinctive from Woo's *A Better Tomorrow* Film Workshop productions as well as *Hard Boiled*, his last Hong Kong film made before leaving for America. After the success of *A Better Tomorrow*, Tsui Hark prevailed upon Woo to make a sequel featuring Cinema City partner Dean Shek. Although he did not want to repeat himself and become trapped in a particular genre, Woo reluctantly agreed to direct this film. He shelved the idea of doing a prequel to *A Better Tomorrow* set in 1970s Vietnam that would show the beginnings of the relationship between Mark and Ho (Ti Lung) established in the earlier film. Following disagreements over the editing of *A Better Tomorrow 2* and Tsui Hark's lack of enthusiasm for *The Killer* project, Woo decided to approach Golden Princess Amusements Company with the support of Chow Yun-fat to make the film that would eventually lead to international recognition and Hollywood contracts for both director and star. Woo later discovered that Tsui Hark intended to make his own version of the prequel titled *A Better Tomorrow 3* that was released in 1989. Since Chow Yun-fat's character died at the end of *A Better Tomorrow*, the original prequel idea appeared to be a good way of bringing the star back to life. Tsui Hark's decision to do his own version of a project he had originally spurned motivated Woo to leave the Film Workshop and become his own producer.[14] Since Woo could not now use Chow Yun-fat in the role he originally envisaged for him as he was now a major star, he decided to cast three young actors then making their names in Hong Kong cinema: Tony Leung Chiu-wai, Jacky Cheung Hok-yau, and Waise Lee (Lei Chi-hung) (Still 1). All were relative "unknowns" at the time and were not major names in the Hong Kong film industry.

Like many Hong Kong actors, Tony Leung began in television under the Hong Kong Television Broadcasts Limited Training Program. He became known for co-hosting a program with Stephen Chow Sing-chi before moving into films and appearing with Chow

Still 1   Tony Leung, Jacky Cheung, and Waise Lee.

Yun-fat in *The Lunatics* (1986), Stanley Kwan's *Love into Waste* (1986), and Hou Hsiao-hsien's Taiwanese production of *City of Sadness* (1989). Despite this promising start, he had not yet become the major star that he would a decade later. By casting him in both *Bullet in the Head* and *Hard Boiled* (1992), John Woo gave this talented actor further recognition and stimulated his future film career in the same way as he had done with Chow Yun-fat. Jacky Cheung began his career as a singer but, like many working in the highly competitive Hong Kong entertainment industry, recognized the importance of diversifying his talents. After gaining a recording contract by winning the 1985 All Hong Kong Singing Contest over ten thousand male competitors, he began learning acting skills and had already received the Hong Kong Film Award for Best Supporting Actor for his role in Wong Kar-wai's *As Tears Go By* (1988). Patrick Leung and John Woo had seen his performance and decided to cast him in the role of Frank which he still regards as his best acting of all his films.[15] By contrast, Waise Lee did not achieve the later star status of his fellow performers. But this is not to deny his essential role in the film. His Paul is an important complement to the characters played by Tony Leung and Jackie Cheung. After beginning his career as a model, his appearance in a television commercial attracted the attention of Tsui Hark (in very much the same way as "Tippi" Hedren came to Alfred Hitchcock's notice) who cast him as the treacherous Shing in *A Better Tomorrow*. Lee's role anticipated his more nuanced performance in *Bullet in the Head* since Woo and Patrick Leung needed the presence of "a calculating traitor who betrays his friends."[16] When making the film, Lee discovered that John Woo did not perform the same type of close mentoring that he had done with him on *A Better Tomorrow*. Instead, by wanting to "create a sad and angry character," the director deliberately isolated Lee from the other actors, preferring to associate with Lee's fellow co-stars, and indulging in behavior reminiscent of John Ford on his worst days on a film set. However, these psychological tactics worked and the actor not only delivered one of the best performances of his career but also individually modeled his climactic manic acting in the closing scenes on Al Pacino's performance in Brian DePalma's *Scarface* (1983). Although Bey Logan expresses frequent criticism of Waise Lee's acting in this film, I disagree with his arguments.[17] Rather than delivering an uncontrolled performance, the actor actually delivers his own version of male hysteria very similar to Al Pacino's role in *Scarface*. His character is an insecure male wishing to overcompensate for his vulnerable personality by acquiring wealth at the cost of betraying his friends. His acting is very much in the tradition of male melodramatic depiction and I will comment further on this later. Lee had already delivered competent performances in 1988 in Kirk Wong's Cinema City production *Gunmen* and Andrew Kam and Johnnie To's *The Big Heat* and would continue to do so after *Bullet in the Head*. He would later play a Triad version of Robert De Niro's Al Capone from Brian De Palma's *The Untouchables* (1987) in David Lam Tak-luk's *First Shot* (1993). Despite his failure to achieve stardom, he is one of Hong Kong cinema's most accomplished character actors.

Other supporting roles deserve attention. Although *Bullet in the Head* is Simon Yam Tat-wah's only role for John Woo to date, his performance as Eurasian assassin Luke is one of the best in his career. Realizing that moving too far away from *A Better Tomorrow*'s romantic overtones into the more "realistic" dimensions of *Bullet in the Head* might alienate audiences, Patrick Leong and Woo decided to cast Yam as a more attractive debonair figure to counterpoint the more "mean streets" characters of the young leading actors. Although Chow Yun-fat's Mark Gor from *A Better Tomorrow* and his Jean-Pierre Melville–influenced "Jeff" of *The Killer* (1989) are missing from *Bullet in the Head*, Yam's accomplished acting style manages both to evoke the aura of this absent figure as well as inflect the role with his own type of distinctive interpretation. Luke's opening appearance belongs amongst the most romantic entries in cinema. With his white suit he evokes the phantom presence of Jeff in *The Killer* as well as expressing Woo's debt to Alain Delon's cool assassin in *Le Samouraï* (1967). The musical leitmotif *Autumn Leaves,* derived from the French version co-written by Jacques Prevert for his 1945 film *Les Portes de la nuit,* announces his presence. Like Jeff, Luke performs a sacrificial act that will redeem his soul from corruption. As Bey Logan points out in his DVD audio-commentary, Luke enters the film physically perfect but inwardly scarred and exits it physically scarred but inwardly purified. Despite his love for Sally (Yolinda Yan Sau-sing), Luke is unable to save her. But, unlike Jeff in *The Killer* who dies at the climax, Luke will live on having gained spiritual salvation by saving Frank and Ben from the Viet Cong prison camp. He becomes a true friend to two Hong Kong street kids who embody values he has long forgotten but which will live on in a disabled body no longer permitting him to continue in his former profession as a hired killer.

Common critical opinion views Woo as a director who cannot satisfactorily depict female performances in his Hong Kong films.

Compared to the four leading characters of *Bullet in the Head*, the roles of Sally and Jane (Fennie Yuen Kit-ying) appear lacking. However, no director is perfect and Woo here exhibits one of his recognizable blind spots. Like Zhang Che, he is more at home depicting the world of men rather than having any type of feminist sensitivity. The female roles are minor. But, nonetheless, they are still important within the structure of *Bullet in the Head*. Now retired from screen, Yolinda Yan was a well-known singer who had earlier appeared in a film by Stanley Kwan titled *The Lying Woman* according to Patrick Leong in a DVD interview. Known for addressing constraining factors governing female experience, Kwan's use of Yolinda Yan in this film probably influenced Woo's casting. Sally undergoes a far worse fate than any of Kwan's heroines. Like Sally Yeh in *The Killer*, she represents a victimized female, symbolizing a lost hope for a return to the safe world of Hong Kong that *Bullet in the Head* reveals as being illusory. None of the three heroes ever returns in the same way. Sally's death represents the final extinction of this romantic hope. Like the wildflower in her song, she is a "dandelion" who will be blown wherever the wind carries her and her fragile persona reflects this. Although she differs from Fennie Yuen, the two women share a basic physical resemblance. Parallels between them occur in the Saigon demonstration scene where her stumbling duplicates the similar movement of Jane during the 1967 Maoist riots outside the Hong Kong factory where she works. Unlike Yolinda Yan, Fennie Yuen's career continued until 2003. Prior to that she had appeared in some key productions such as Sammo Hung Kam-po's accomplished action-comedy-drama *Pedicab Driver* (1986), Ringo Lam's *School on Fire* (1988), Lau Kar-leung's final installment of the *Aces Go Places* series — *Aces Go Places V: The Terracotta Hit* (1989), and Tsui Hark's troubled Film Workshop production *Swordsman* (1990) which also featured a score by *Bullet in the Head* composers James Wong Jin and Romeo Diaz. As Jane, Fennie

Yuen mostly displays those token submissive qualities of a heroine from a Zhang Che film where emphasis lies on heroes rather than heroines. Hers is a thankless role. But Jane does display resilience by questioning Ben's illusions that their separation will be temporary before he departs for Saigon. In the midst of the Maoist demonstration and imminent bomb explosion, she punctuates his earlier fantasy of flying away somewhere free from historical and political violence. "The whole world is in turmoil. Who knows what tomorrow will bring?" Jane is more realistic about the future than her newly wed husband.

Last, but not least, credit should go to the menacing performance of Lam Chung as Chinese-Vietnamese Triad boss Mr. Leong. As Larry Cohen once told me, any good film needs a great villain and Lam Chung superbly fills this category. He is very underrated in Hong Kong cinema and his achievements deserve special mention. This well-known (to Hong Kong audiences) prolific actor-director had appeared in Tony Au Ding-ping's reincarnation feature *Dream Lovers* (1986) as a reformed thief now working as a museum curator, Ronny Yu Yan-tai's *Legacy of Rage* (1986), *Angel* (1987), Sun Chung's overwrought melodrama *Lady in Black* (1987), *A Better Tomorrow 2* (1987), Taylor Wong Tai-loi and Johnny Mak's production *Rich and Famous* (1987), Tony Leung Si-hung's sequel *Tragic Hero* (1987) playing a Triad in both films, Jeff Lau Chun-wai's female *Police Academy* spin-off *Operation Pink Squad* (1988), David Lam's *Call Girl* (1988), Lowell Lo Kwung-ting's female prison drama *The First Time Is the Last Time* (1989), Wong Chung's comedy *Run Don't Walk* (1989), Yuen Bun's *A Moment of Romance* (1990), and Na Nai-choi's *Erotic Ghost Story* (1990). A year after *Bullet in the Head* Lam Chung would portray a Japanese mad scientist sexual sadist in Jaimie Luk Kim-ming's cult classic *Robotrix* (1991).

John Woo probably cast him as Mr. Leong due to his gangster role in *A Better Tomorrow 2* and as Chow Yun-fat's first victim in the opening scenes of *The Killer*. But Lam Chung could also portray other characters such as policemen in Clifton Ko Chi-sum's 1986 drama *Devoted to You* (which also starred Jackie Cheung), Che-Kirk Wong's remake of *Angels with Dirty Faces* now set in 1955 Hong Kong — *True Colours* (1986) with Ti Lung in the James Cagney role, Tony Au's 1935 period prostitution drama *Profiles of Pleasure* (1988), Yuen Cheung-yan's 1989 drama *Live Hard* (starring Simon Yam), Alfred Cheung Kin-ting's pre-Handover satire *Her Fatal Ways* (1990), Norman Law-man's *Family Honor* (1990), and even a film director in Anthony Chan-yau's romantic comedy drama *A Fishy Story* (1989)! Since many Hong Kong films such as Kirk Wong's *Organized Crime and Triad Bureau* (1994) and the *Infernal Affairs* trilogy deal with criminal activities in the police force, it is not surprising that Lam Chung often portrays characters on both sides of the law. As Bey Logan remarks on the audio-commentary of the 2004 *Hong Kong Legends* DVD release of *Bullet in the Head*, Lam Chung's character represents a composite version based on actual characters in the Hong Kong film industry whether gangster and/or businessmen. Any producer or director knows that appropriate casting is essential to any film's success especially involving a good villain. Lam Chung admirably fills that category in his role as Mr. Leong. Furthermore, whether John Woo knew this or not, the actor had also appeared in Zhang Che's *One Armed Swordsman*. Another coincidental Zhang Che association occurred in the casting of Pau Hei-ching as Ben's mother. Still working today, she began her career during the 1950s and 60s working at Zhang Che's old studio Cheung Sing/Great Wall known for its Cantonese social melodramas in the various capacities of actress, assistant, and script-girl. Her brief appearances playing Ben's more sympathetic mother, juxtaposed with Paul's bitter father, would add a particular resonance to the earlier scenes in *Bullet in the Head* that showed the last days of this rapidly vanishing Hong Kong working-class community.

This very ambitious project demanded a large budget. Since he was still under contract with the Film Workshop, Terence Chang could not work as producer with Woo until *Hard Boiled*.[18] The film's cost rose from HKD 8 million to 28 million, a huge sum at that time. As opposed to the normal two-to-three-month shooting schedule, *Bullet in the Head* took five months to make with location scenes in Thailand substituting for Vietnam. The interiors were shot in Hong Kong studios with special location scenes sct in rapidly disappearing council home tenement buildings as well as those remaining World War II air-raid shelters. John Woo's most ambitious and creative project was about to begin: an epic period war film that deliberately differed from the director's two previously successful breakthrough gangster films. As Bey Logan states, "*Bullet in the Head* aimed at a David Lean epic quality without a David Lean budget." John Woo began to fulfill a dream that had earlier influenced his desire to make films by finally directing his own version of a David Lean epic that would be much darker in tone. However, like all his other cinematic influences whether Western (Melville, Peckinpah, Scorsese) or East Asian (Zhang Che, Kurosawa), he would make *Bullet in the Head* his own personal project and unique creation as "A John Woo Production."[19]

2

Bullet in the Head

John Woo's epic production of *Bullet in the Head* belongs amongst Hong Kong cinema's finest achievements. It is not an exclusively violent film but operates on more than one level. *Bullet in the Head* is a film deserving detailed close reading and meticulous analysis not only to reveal its inherent difference from the majority of Hong Kong action films but also to show its true nature as a serious work of tragic dimensions. Woo's masterpiece has claims to be seen as both an accomplished Hong Kong film as well as a major achievement of contemporary cinema. It demands more meticulous attention than it has previously received.

Woo's critical reputation has usually suffered from overemphasis on the violent scenes in his films. However, more intuitive explorations of those important themes existing within the generic formulas that he both employs and changes significantly are urgently needed. As well as developing the director's stylistic signatures such as balletic violence and refined action sequences, previously seen in his *A Better Tomorrow* films and *The Killer*,

Bullet in the Head is an accomplished work in terms of its screenplay structure involving significantly integrated components. It demonstrates the classical elements of a "well made play" beginning with a prologue (now confined to the credit sequences) and concluding with an epilogue depicting the revenge that Ben must undertake to give rest both to Frank's soul as well as end the contamination that has affected virtually every character in the film.[1]

Within these framing contexts of prologue and epilogue, *Bullet in the Head* parallels a four-act structure of a classical play. This is not accidental. The first part depicts the unity between three friends in Hong Kong and the challenges presented by violence and exile from their homeland. During the second part, the even more violent environment of Vietnam presents greater challenges to their unity as Paul becomes more infected by his greedy desires for gold while Ben, Frank, and Luke attempt in vain to rescue Sally from the savage nature of a landscape that now represents a hellish contemporary version of that demonic wilderness seen in those Puritan Captivity narratives that influenced American literature and cinema. The third act opens with the three heroes experiencing their version of a "Season in Hell" within a Viet Cong prison camp. This also represents one version of Hong Kong's worst nightmare following the 1989 events in Tiananmen Square and dark forebodings concerning what might happen in 1997. It moves towards Luke's rescue of his friends, the final corruption of Paul, his deadly betrayal of Frank and Ben, the rescue of Ben by Buddhist monks, and his return to Hong Kong. Although this last segment could suggest a particular type of happy ending where an emotionally scarred veteran might settle down in peace with his family, any optimistic resolution is impossible. Ben cannot deny the traumatic effects of his recent historical past. Debts need to be paid and a deceased friend revenged so that his spirit may finally rest. This occurs in the final act of the drama of a film which opens with a prologue depicting the early life of the main characters and concludes in a poignant epilogue leaving one solitary and emotionally scarred survivor as dawn breaks. His experiences resemble that other solitary survivor at the end of Herman Melville's *Moby Dick* who lives to tell the tale. The former bond between three young men is now definitively broken. One lies dead and another's skull lies in the center of flames ironically evoking a funeral pyre for a tormented spirit finally given rest. Even though Ben escapes the law, he will be contaminated forever by the violence he has witnessed in the past and the final reckoning he has had to perform in the present.

Woo's apocalyptic melodrama is a Chinese version of a revenge tragedy as bloody and as compelling as its Jacobean counterparts. *Bullet in the Head*'s closest parallel is *Blood Brothers*, a film Woo worked on as an assistant director for Zhang Che. Ma Sin (Ti Lung) has betrayed Wang Chung (Chen Kuan-tai) after he has also seduced his wife. Chang Wen (David Chiang Wei-nien) now has to take revenge on a treacherous blood brother. He eventually succeeds in his quest but finally faces execution after his judicial examination. Chang Wen knows that his fate is inescapable. Like the earlier Kuan character he played in *Vengeance* (1970), David Chiang knows that he will never survive at the end of a bloody contest. In *Vengeance*, Ti Lung played the victimized (and literal) blood brother. By contrast, he now plays the victimizer in *Blood Brothers*. In *Blood Brothers*, the Chen Kuan-tai and David Chiang characters are lower-class outlaws quite happy to remain in their positions in life until Ti Lung's more unscrupulous Ma Sing takes them under his wing and teaches them martial arts. He uses them to facilitate his rise to power in the Imperial Chinese establishment. In *Bullet in the Head*, Ben (Tony Leung Chiu-wai) and Frank (Jackie Cheung Hok-yau) appear content with their lives. Although Ben daydreams about flying away like a bird, his aspirations are idealistic and unrealistic as Jane (Fenny Yuen Kit-ying) recognizes. He would never do anything to injure his friends. On the other hand, although he is not a member of the upper classes like Ma Sin, Paul (Waise Lee Chi-hung) is downwardly mobile and resents it. He can never forget the previous exalted status of his father as an officer in the pre-1949 Chinese Nationalist Army, a father who constantly urges him to get ahead without ever cautioning him about what this might cost in terms of honor and personal values. Friendship, loyalty, and the revenge of betrayal are key concepts within those knightly ideals found in Chinese classical literature from *The Water Margin* and *Romance of the Three Kingdoms* onwards. They occur in various forms throughout the different narratives of the later *wuxia* literary tradition and its cinematic recreation in the work of Zhang Che and others. In *A Better Tomorrow*, Woo adapts these values to the changed world of the gangster film, sympathizing with their modern ephemeral status while at the same time fully conscious of the fact that they represent one of those many things "in danger of being lost" within the changing society of Hong Kong.

Although John Charles, Bey Logan, and other critics believe that the changed ending in the boardroom where Ben kills his nemesis represents a more appropriate conclusion for the film "that needed to end on a whimper and not a bang," by contrast I feel that the supposedly redundant climax contained in most circulating copies of the film represents an appropriate climax.[2] Ben has returned to Hong Kong. He must avenge the death of his friend. The final battle occurs in an apocalyptic manner evoking not only the hellish environment of Vietnam but also underscoring the personally traumatic nature of a revenge Ben must undertake to fulfill his obligations of friendship to the betrayed Frank. Although these lower-class youngsters are far removed from those past heroes of *wuxia* literature and films as well as their modern counterparts in the *A Better Tomorrow* series, they share many of the values of their predecessors — with the notable exception of Paul who exhibits discontent with ideals he regards as outmoded from the very beginning of the film. He is Woo's version, conscious or not, of John Milton's Lucifer in *Paradise Lost.* Although he does not revolt against any deity, he is fully aware of his father's fall from institutional grace and seeks to regain the economic status his family once had in pre-Maoist China. ("Evil, be thou my good.") While Ben and Frank share common values of friendship and loyalty, Paul seeks material advantage from the very beginning of the film. He hopes to be a "big timer" in Hong Kong society. Paul falls from a collective lower-class realm offering him friendship and solidarity into his own personal hell of individual capitalist acquisitiveness. His youthful existence may be "far from heaven" but it offers him more choices than his eventual road to damnation will.

Bullet in the Head also understands that it is impossible to return to the past. Woo reveals that changes are already affecting Hong Kong in 1967 that will make any return to those old social values of 1950s Cantonese cinema represented by films such as Lee Tit's *Space is Gold* (1950), *In the Face of Demolition*, and the various versions of *The House of 72 Tenants* (1963, 1973) impossible. The youngsters exist in a changed world where parents engage in gambling and male dancers move from church halls to gang fights overlooking Hong Kong Bay. Strikers, baton-wielding police, and Maoist demonstrators act as disruptive features of a changed universe. Nothing can ever be the same again. The bleak climax of the film emphasizes this.

Prologue

Bullet in the Head's opening credit sequence employs that famous 1960s musical theme representing the greatest hit of The Monkees — "I'm A Believer." Woo's use of this period pop song is not merely nostalgic since it occurs during different parts of the film to accompany different types of sequences. It most notably

reoccurs in the restroom sequence of the Bolero Club where Ben
and Luke (Simon Yam Tat-wah) meet for the first time and
intuitively recognize each other's real character before Luke's bloody
assassination of a greedy South Vietnamese customs official. The
theme sets the period agenda of a film whose credits begin with "A
John Woo Production" before featuring those three young then
unknowns as stars by means of graphic imagery before displaying
several crayon drawings that initially appear irrelevant (Still 2).[3]
However, these drawings actually represent modern versions of
those traditional calligraphy representations introducing King Hu
films such as *The Fate of Lee Khan* (1973) and *The Valiant Ones*
(1974) that supply contextual details for successive scenes. They
also display important visual information relevant to significant
themes within *Bullet in the Head*. These illustrations employ key
primary colors that reoccur throughout the film such as red and
yellow. One drawing briefly occupies the entire screen before it
dissolves into two succeeding images each divided into four
segments. The first illustration reveals a cross on a thatched roof
while the second dissolves to a cross on the top left graphic before
another dissolve reveals another cross on the bottom right image.
A key Woo visual icon appears on the bottom left graphic in this
third and final dissolve. It shows doves flying across a red sunset.
The doves symbolize peace. They also occur in Woo's Hong Kong
(*The Killer*) and Hollywood films (*Face/Off*).

Woo's use of "I'm a Believer" represents neither his utilitarian
use of background music culled from the soundtrack library nor a
mere signifier of period detail. It contains important levels of
meaning juxtaposing what people think they believe in throughout
the film. But an apocalyptic world of violence surrounds them
wherever they are. Although misleadingly stereotyped as a "master
of violence" in the same way as Sam Peckinpah, Woo's films often
contain alternative elements opposing the brutality of a destructive
world order. Like Peckinpah, Woo never didactically displays key

Still 2   Woo's modern version of King Hu's calligraphy.

meanings but expects viewers to discern them on their own. They exist inside the text in the same way as that idyllic desert Edenic harmony between Cable and Hildy in *The Ballad of Cable Hogue* (1970) and the utopian Mexican village of *The Wild Bunch* (1969). The first represents an alternative to Cable's desire for revenge and capitalist greed while the second represents a lost world for the Bunch but one that will forever celebrate those tarnished Americans as posthumous heroes within the realm of legend as the final credit sequences show. *Bullet in the Head*'s opening images reveal countryside locations. But any return to a pastoral world Lee Tit earlier presented as a viable option to Hong Kong's greedy and selfish city in his South China Film Worker's Union production of *Space Is Gold* (1950) becomes entirely impossible. Instead *Bullet*'s countryside represents another deadly example of the Vietnamese apocalypse rather than the idyllic pastoral alternative presented by *Space Is Gold*. But this landscape also contains Buddhist monks who rescue Ben despite the fact that their agency is marginalized by new historical forces. Like the image of the cross seen in these drawings and the one situated in the background of the church hall in the opening scenes, Woo suggests that alternatives exist for those wishing to seek them.

As the credits roll, the next sequences show Ben acting as dance instructor inside a church hall as the "I'm a Believer" theme continues (Still 3). Although truncated from the far more detailed version envisaged by Woo, these scenes reveal adolescent playfulness manifested in a harmless dance as Ben applies his talents in more positive ways than his later outside role as "Leader of the Pack." He is a natural director as his mastery of ballroom dancing, the Tango, and the Twist reveals. The equation between the cross in the background and the use of "I'm a Believer" suggests a more positive display of adolescent energy as opposed to its more violent manifestations in the *West Side Story*–inspired "Rumble" sequence outside the church hall. Both these movements by Ben are meticulously choreographed. It is no secret that Woo often stages his fight sequences in the same way as dance routines in a Hollywood musical. The brief church hall sequence is also the nearest approximation to Richard Dyer's definition of the musical in terms of the utopian dimensions of entertainment.[4] Like the classical Hollywood musical, this sequence reveals a brief utopian sensibility in terms of offering a temporary escape from outside problems of existence in the same way as the opening dance sequence of *A Better Tomorrow 2* (1987). Ben and his fellow dancers are lower-class Hong Kong youngsters finding pleasure in

Still 3   Entertainment as utopia — the dance hall.

Still 4   Ben as dance director.

an "invitation to the dance" offered by the church hall allowing them to engage harmlessly in the youthful vitality of 60s rock and roll culture (Still 4). During two shots in this dance sequence, the camera moves from left to right. It conducts a circular movement in another brief shot representing the positive nature of youthful vitality and Ben's peaceful role as director within this harmonious world. However, these positive alternatives face deadly challenges outside. The following "Rumble" sequence demonstrates this. Choreographed in a manner resembling the battle between the Sharks and the Jets in Robert Wise's *West Side Story* (1961), "I'm a Believer" again reoccurs but this time as a more ironic overture. These dance movements are much more serious and deadly than those inside the church hall. Indeed, one brief shot of the earlier dance sequence revealed Ben briefly pausing as if he has suffered injury from a wound in some earlier violent confrontation. When he appears on the scene leading Frank and Paul against Ringo (Yee Tin Hung/Paco Yick) and his gang, Ben now directs a much more violent dance. He appears instrumental in helping his friends to victory against their opponents. In these opening scenes Woo presents Ben as torn between two types of belief: utopian harmony and aggressive violence whose implications will become tragically apparent in the later part of the film.

Before showing Ben's victory, Woo interrupts the fight by inserting two reflective scenes revealing a contrast between Ben and Paul. Following the Twist sequence in the church hall, an abrupt cut shows Ben combing his hair in the mirror in an attempt to style his hair like Elvis Presley whose photo appears on the wall opposite that of John F. Kennedy.[5] But the cut actually begins by showing Ben running a tap over his head in his bathroom, an action that Frank duplicates later after his confrontation with Ringo when he attempts to remove traces of blood from his head. Even these early scenes suggest that this blood brotherhood existing between two friends will take on more deadly overtones in Vietnam. The image of Elvis lap-dissolves to a close-up of Ben as his mother comments on his fascination with Western popular culture. Woo then cuts to another photo on a wall. This time it is Paul's father. Formerly a senior officer in the pre-1949 Chinese Nationalist Army, he is now reduced to being a road sweeper in Hong Kong. He reflects on his current humiliating status to Paul. "It's a cruel world. Money talks! Without it, you're shit. If you get a break, hang in there." Paul's apartment also has an American icon: a poster of the famous photograph revealing the raising of the flag at Iwo Jima. As well as representing a key representation of American superiority towards the end of World War II, the image is also a symbol of post-war American military power. The U.S. Army won the battle against heavily outnumbered Japanese defenders due to its superior manpower and weapons, a strategy existing from the days of Sherman, Pershing, and Patton etc. onwards. American weaponry and fascination with powerful weapons will influence Paul in Saigon. America is also associated with material wealth. As a failed pawn in American Cold War economic support of Nationalist China, Paul's father understands the lesson of failure. He is determined that his son will not become another loser and has obviously drilled this into Paul's mind several times. By contrast, Ben follows an America represented by the idealistic image of John F. Kennedy and the effervescent, vibrant image of Elvis Presley before induction into the Army and change into a corporate product via the machinations of Colonel Tom Parker would lead to ignominious decline as an overweight Las Vegas entertainer. Both these brief scenes employ a wistful rendition of the main "*Bullet in the Head*" theme that occurs in significant parts of the film rather than "I'm a Believer."

During the first part of the fight Frank is instantly recognizable (Still 5). But he is clearly no match for Ringo. Woo then inserts another scene revealing Frank as a gentle character flying a kite to attract a young girl on a tenement balcony and forgetting his role as look-out for his parents' illegal gambling activities. When the police arrive and arrest his father, Frank's angry mother beats him on the head with a slipper, another ominous foreshadowing of a more deadly incident that will occur later in the film. As opposed to Ben's mother, she is far less gentle and more mercenary like Paul's father. Woo then returns to the fight accompanied again by "I'm a Believer," obviously intended to contrast two different worlds of peace and violence. Ben's arrival changes the course of the battle. He hits Ringo, employs the use of a bicycle chain wrapped around his hand (seen in close-up), and holds a knife to his defeated opponent's throat. Although choreographed in a rapid breath-taking manner, these fights reveal a violent streak in Ben's character that may destroy him.

Still 5 Frank provokes his antagonist — East Side Story.

After the fight, the three friends walk together in a lower-class area of Hong Kong. Frank briefly plays with a child. When they see children playing with a skipping rope, they all successively participate in the activity. A series of lap dissolves shows them all joining in a harmless game. It is the penultimate moment for all three to be seen united together as friends enjoying one form of "harmless entertainment" that is not life-threatening.[6] Woo later shows them again together for the last time after Ben's wedding banquet by using his characteristic freeze frame device to emphasize a poignant moment. Their friendship will soon be destroyed by forces beyond their control. Woo's characters live in a historically unstable world opposing any forms of peaceful and personal fulfillment.

Romance also offers no real alternative especially since Hong Kong society now faces a world of political chaos. Woo introduces Jane in close-up as she moves in slow motion to a lush theme song evocative of the Liverpool sound of Billy J. Kramer's "Do You Want to Know a Secret?" written by the Beatles songwriting team of John Lennon and Paul McCartney. When Ben begins his romantic overtures to Jane outside the factory where she works, a group of agitators begin leafleting the employees. Their activities ominously foreshadow other more violent demonstrations later in the film. A year after the 1966 Star Ferry riots, Maoist demonstrators began more violent forms of protest and the opening scenes of the film echo this climate. One of the leaflets reads "Long Live Chairman Mao." The police intervene and arrest the demonstrators. Woo then reveals the date with the caption "Hong Kong 1967," the year the colony nearly approached civil insurgency. Ben's courtship of Jane begins amidst these turbulent conditions. A later sequence showing a much more violent demonstration shows their separation following the death of Ringo.[7] The prologue to the film succinctly reveals that all the major characters are trapped in historical events, giving their individual dilemmas an epic dimension. Woo now begins his own Hong Kong version of a David Lean epic. At the end of the film everyone will become traumatically affected by historical events in the same way as characters in *Lawrence of Arabia* (1962) and *Dr. Zhivago* (1965). Nothing will ever be the same again.

Part One

After introducing the main principals in the prologue and hinting at elements that will reoccur in more deadly forms later, *Bullet in the Head* moves towards Act One. It begins at night with Paul sitting alone outside the small business premises of Jane's family that viewers will see later at the beginning of Act Four when Ben returns home. As opposed to the gang fight, skipping rope sequences, and the end of Ben's wedding night banquet where Paul is part of a closely knit trio, he now sits apart from his friends. This is the first of many sequences where Woo places some distance between Paul and his friends. It begins with the camera tracking right to left framing him sitting at a table. Across the street, one of the buildings reveals the ominous number "13." Paul broods about his social position and feels he is going nowhere. Like Ben, he wishes to leave for another destination but his desires are less utopian and more material. Thinking of his father's fate, he wishes to pursue the Hong Kong material dream of upward mobility. Sensing Paul's deep unhappiness, the gentle Frank attempts to comfort him. "Wherever you go, count us in. We're all orphans here." He also describes them as "wildflowers" going "where the wind blows us." His lines not only describe their feelings but also evoke the lyrics of a popular Cantonese song later sung by Sally (Yolinda Yan Choh-sin) who by this time is a drug-addicted sex slave in Saigon. She will sing this song later in the Bolero night club sequence when Mr. Y. S. Leong (Lam Chung) bullies the young men. The lines evoke those dark ironic connotations of the eternal Chinese diaspora dilemma in a colony facing an unknown future. Contemporary feelings existing at the time of the making of *Bullet in the Head* play an influential role in this scene that evokes not just that turbulent 1966–67 era, which saw social unrest in Hong Kong and the acceleration of the Vietnam War affecting both Vietnamese and Chinese (as Ann Hui On-wah's 1981 *The Story of Woo Viet* and her 1982 *The Boat People* show) but also a post–Tiananmen Square climate that created shock waves throughout the colony. These historical and future perfect references suggest that Frank expresses false optimism concerning their supposed freedom of movement. Although Woo may never have read Dostoevsky's *The Idiot*, Frank's character has many parallels to the saintly Prince Myshkin as well as those noble street kids seen in 1950s Cantonese melodramas and later films such as Lo Wei's *Back Alley Princess* (1973). Paul reveals his desire to return to Hong Kong in a Mercedes (which he eventually does drive in the film's concluding scenes). Frank then replies, "Let's not wait. Let's drive a Mercedes now." He gently wishes to indulge the fantasy of a friend whom he feels will never escape Hong Kong's mean streets. But his suggestion also has dark consequences. It fuels Paul's desire to compete and succeed at all costs.

The succeeding bicycle race between the three friends shows them again united as in the skipping rope scene (Still 6). As in that earlier scene, it employs the same lyrical rendering of the film's main musical theme evoking the harmless nature of adolescent unity. However, Paul turns the bike ride into a competition between himself and his two friends so that he will emerge the winner. He no longer plays in unity with his friends as he did earlier in the skipping rope scene but changes a friendly game into an individualist form of competition aiming to be number one. He challenges Ben, "I'm always a winner," as the three cycle towards the edge of the docks in Woo's own version of the chicken run from *Rebel without a Cause* (1955). Ben and Paul reach the edge

Still 6 The bicycle race.

of the dock in safety but Frank topples over and is helped to safety by Ben. When Woo repeats this race in the epilogue, he films Frank's fall in slow motion. This technical device also makes the audience remember that Paul held his hands high up in the air to denote victory in the earlier scene. This act reveals his egocentric nature since he shows no concern for Frank falling over the side. By contrast, Ben makes no such gesture and this allows him to be in a better position to rescue his friend from falling into the water. As they walk away, Frank sings the words of a local song, "Punk in the gutter," anticipating the same type of humor that he will employ when he returns with a bleeding head to Ben's wedding banquet with the money. Ironically, Frank later becomes a deadly Saigon punk in the gutter during later poignant sequences in the film.

Reality soon begins to cast ominous shadows over the carefree nature of these early scenes where nothing seems to matter and a violent fight resembles a Hollywood musical more than a life-threatening incident. Fantasies soon become more deadly. Before Ben proposes to Jane, he reveals to her his desire to fly away like a bird and even imitates one. They both walk outside dilapidated Hong Kong factory buildings whose presence ominously foreshadows developing changes in the economy from a manufacturing to the high technological entity of today. Ben is much more carefree in this scene. He reveals his gentle nature to Jane in much the same way as Frank did when attempting to impress a young girl by flying a kite in the prologue that eventually landed in the gutter like the punk in the song. "There are great places out there. It's my ambition. Most people do not even have that." However, flight is an impossible goal for human beings unless it embodies non-material, transcendent dimensions. Woo's doves seen in one of the drawings introducing the film and in that peaceful flight of white birds that Ben later observes when he recovers in the Buddhist sanctuary symbolize this concept. As a poor working-class woman, Jane worries about the financial barriers hindering Ben's proposal. "We're poor. How can we get money for our wedding?" During the 1950s and 60s, marriage was a communal celebration involving the participation of the entire community rather than members of the immediate family. Such economic obstacles appear insurmountable. At that time, it would take many years to raise the money for this type of huge celebration.

Due to producer demands many scenes were eliminated from this part of the film. Several of these involved detailed depictions of lower class life that could have explained why Ben and Jane suddenly triumph over economic adversity. Similar abrupt transitions also occur elsewhere in the film due to hasty editing decisions. After Jane voices her concerns, Woo cuts to a close-up of the bride wearing traditional red regalia representing the lost world of the Mainland that many of these people left from 1949 onwards. Despite the fact that Ben teaches dancing in a church hall and may be part of the colony's Christian community (as was Woo at the time), he and his bride respect traditional Chinese customs. Jane wears a traditional red costume. She does not wear a white wedding dress as many Hong Kong women did from the 1980s onwards. These early scenes show a Hong Kong community that is slowly disappearing. It is a world familiar to viewers of 1960s and 70s Hong Kong cinema where Chinese traditional values were still strong. Other missing scenes may have contained similar features. During Jane's wedding, everyone in the council house area appears involved in one way or another. These brief images represent another example of Woo's concern about important Hong Kong social traditions in danger of becoming lost in a rapidly changing society.

How does the wedding go ahead? Missing scenes may have revealed Ben's unhappiness over lack of money and Frank's willingness to help him achieve his romantic goal. What scenes remain in the film show how Frank does this? The surviving footage does not supply much information as to the exact way he raises the money. But the audience can guess when they see the later scene of Frank being thrown out of his family home with little explanation given in the dialogue. The original version of the film probably supplied details that Frank used the deeds to his parents' apartment as security for a loan he obtained from Mr. Kwai (Raymond Lee Wai-man).

The current version of the film immediately moves into the wedding sequence with Ben, Jane, and Frank appearing as component parts of this collective gathering. By contrast, Paul appears more isolated from a community he feels little connection with. One scene shows him seated alongside local businessmen with underworld associations. Rather than rejoicing in his friend's wedding, he is more interested in material gain. He asks Mr. Shing how to make money. The businessman draws his attention to the chaotic situation of Vietnam and advises him to take risks. "The more chaos: the easier the cash. Anything goes to make a buck. A lot of millionaires started out this way." Morality does not enter into this type of advice favoring capitalist exploitation rather than Confucian values of collective humanitarianism. We do not know who has arranged this wedding banquet. However, the context here suggests that Paul has approached Mr. Shing after Frank has guaranteed getting the money. Why else would Shing and his business associate be present at a lower-class event? Paul later anxiously approaches his friends. "The boss is getting impatient. Got it?" He looks at Frank who gives him the money which he passes to a caterer.

Frank temporarily leaves the wedding celebrations to contact loan shark Mr. Kwai. During this sequence, it rains constantly. Rain represents a sign of good fortune in Chinese tradition. But it also can express ominous references to those dangerous rainy sequences in Kurosawa films such as *The Seven Samurai* and *Ran*. Frank's obtaining the money is an act of good fortune. But, by engaging in an act of generosity for a close friend, he sets into motion a chain of deadly incidents that will escalate into apocalyptic dimensions. Money causes the first accidental killing in the film. It later inspires a more deliberate act of murder by Paul. Dressed in his street clothes, Frank waits for Mr. Kwai. As he does so, Woo uses the first of his significant dissolve sequences. Frank looks at a sign hanging over the restaurant. The Chinese characters mean "Double Happiness." The sign lap-dissolves to a slow-motion shot of the happy couple before dissolving to a close-up of Frank. "Double Happiness" would primarily signify Ben and Jane whose marital happiness Frank has done his utmost to achieve. But by dissolving back to a close-up of Frank, Woo demonstrates that his understanding of double happiness also involves Frank. Like a hero from traditional Cantonese and Mandarin melodramas, Frank sacrifices himself to ensure the good fortune of those he loves. He shares in the happiness of a friend who has married the woman of his choice without having to wait many years for this to happen. This will result in final rejection by his parents. Frank's form of lower-class sacrifice lacks the moralistic dimensions of traditional Confucian Chinese culture. He has, after all, used his family's apartment deeds as security for a loan without telling them. However, Frank's act represents the highest form of sacrifice that he can make within his own social structure according to values he believes are important. But it will have dark repercussions involving violence and death.

After getting the money from Mr. Kwai, Frank again encounters Ringo and his gang. They now wish to avenge their humiliating defeat seen earlier in the pre-credits sequence. Frank attempts to leave in vain. "I'll fight you again one day." But Ringo knows Frank has seen Mr. Kwai and brutally hits him on the head with a bottle. Frank struggles to get the money back. This occurs in a rapidly edited sequence of action shots. Woo uses two significant close-ups here. One emphasizes Ringo's bottle smashing Frank's head and causing "first blood" in the film. The other reveals Frank's borrowed money in Ringo's hand before Frank retrieves it and runs away. These close-ups reinforce the deadly combination of money and violence structuring the narrative of *Bullet in the Head*. Money is a force that will ruin lives and breach close bonds of friendship.

After Frank returns to give the money to Paul, Woo uses three significant close-up shots. The first reveals a concerned Ben looking at Frank seeing through the clownish persona his friend adopts to distract people's attention from his serious injury. The second close-up shows blood still flowing from Frank's wound despite his brief attempt to wash it away. A third close-up again shows Ben recognizing that Frank has suffered an injury on his behalf. Paul is notably absent from these shots. They parallel those earlier "Double Happiness" dissolves linking Ben and Frank but not Paul. He is never really part of this close bonding despite the formal gestures of friendship he chooses to make. Woo's direction and Waise Lee's performance in these key Hong Kong scenes suggest that Paul is more of an alienated character than the other two. Differences already exist between Paul and his friends long before his contamination by gold in Leong's Saigon nightclub. Unlike Ben, Paul shows little concern for his friend's condition. He becomes impatient with Frank and asks for money to repay the debt owed for the wedding celebration. By contrast, Ben sees through the comic performance Frank displays to conceal his pain. Frank again sings the "Punk in the gutter" song. Money makes him a "punk in the gutter" during Ringo's attack. It will do so again in a more devastating manner later in the film.

Woo thus develops his apocalyptic melodrama in the best manner of any classical tragedy, showing the beginning of a process that will lead to damnation for these three young men. He ends the wedding sequence with freeze frame imagery inherited from Zhang Che. But he applies his own creative interpretation to reveal contradictory overtones contained within the image. The three friends unite together for what will prove to be the last time. They are shot closely together. Frank is at the center with Ben on his left and Paul on his right (Still 7). Triangular groupings featuring this trio frequently occur throughout *Bullet in the Head* but with significant variations progressively revealing Paul becoming more isolated from the other two. Frank appropriately occupies the heart of the group. With his demise, the moral center of the film will disappear leaving the other two in an alienated and antagonistic moral vacuum. The final lines spoken before the freeze frame

Still 7 Three friends together — for the last time.

articulate the egalitarian nature of true friendship that will soon vanish. Paul understands friendship in a more hierarchical manner involving a boss or "big brother" at the top as his lines denote. Ben rejects this definition. "What's this boss crap? You two are my big brothers. We're buddies and buddies are equal." The image then freezes showing the three friends united resembling an old family photo that survives the ravages and time while those displayed within it do not. It is a very poignant shot. Woo then fades the image to black acknowledging that this freeze frame represents an image of a past forever lost.

Revenge and Exile

The next sequence shows Ben, his back to the camera. He smokes a cigarette at night, taking a break from his marital duties. Due to the nature of the council estate where he lives, no real privacy is possible. He sees Frank being ejected from his parents' apartment and discovers how he obtained the money for the wedding banquet. Ben now owes his friend a debt of brotherhood and he has no hesitation as to how he will pay it. Disbelieving Frank's explanation of an accidental fall, he slams his own head against the wall and receives just a bruise rather than the blood he earlier saw flowing from his friend's head when he arrived with the money. Despite Frank's protestations, "I'm not bleeding but it hurts," the two friends decide to take street revenge on Ringo. A close-up shows the bottles they will employ in a street fight. It parallels that earlier close-up showing the bottle Ringo used on Frank's head. The image also emphasizes a further escalation of violence that began as a dance routine during the credit sequences. It will now take on more dangerous overtones. These bottles differ from those knightly weapons used in a Zhang Che *wuxia* film. But times have changed. Woo's choice of this close-up emphasizes the ominous nature of the decision Ben and Frank make. By employing the same weapons as Ringo they become little better than him. Ben and Frank will later use more deadly weapons to kill unarmed prisoners in the Viet Cong camp. Like Howard Hawks, Woo uses close-ups sparingly to emphasize a strategic moment in the narrative. In *Rio Bravo*, Hawks uses an abrupt close-up in the prologue to emphasize the moment when Joe Burdett's decision to use a gun will change the lives of all concerned. It follows that previous climactic close-up that emphasized the challenging moment of the coin dropping into the spittoon that may accelerate Dude's final degradation.[8] By contrast, *Bullet in the Head* uses more close-ups in its opening act to emphasize dangerous elements of blood, money, and weapons that will take on more apocalyptic manifestations as the film develops.

The next sequence shows the two friends approaching Ringo's "turf." Their unaware victim relaxes by smoking dope. Were this a Zhang Che or traditional *wuxia* narrative Ben and Frank would allow their opponent time to recover his senses before engaging in mortal combat. But such traditions no longer exist. The *West Side Story* borrowings of *Bullet in the Head*'s credit sequences become even more ominous. Ben again takes command by silently motioning Frank to move to another position. The "Leader of the Pack" now uses his skill as a dance hall instructor to teach his friend the appropriate steps he needs for this more violent ballet. Battle then commences. Choreographed by Lau Chi-ho, the fighting is exhilarating with rapid editing and meticulously planned movements representing the best traditions of Hong Kong action cinema. However, despite the excitement, this battle is not without its contradictory features. Unlike Frank in the earlier fight sequence, Ben now begins the invitation to this deadly dance. Although Ben wishes to avenge his friend's violent humiliation as a matter of honor, he is drawn into a circuit of violence that will accelerate beyond control before the film concludes.

Ben hits Ringo on the head with a bottle. So does Frank. On re-mastered DVD versions of *Bullet in the Head*, the vibrant music score by Wong and Diaz begins at this crucial moment. It continues to follow the action during the rest of the fight and winds down at the point when Ben sees Ringo's dead body. He stabs Ringo by thrusting a knife in his leg. This action not only anticipates the later crippling of Leong in Saigon by bullets but also Ben's shooting Paul in the leg during their final battle. Ben batters Ringo's head with a brick several times. His actions anticipate the manner he will later repeatedly fire bullets into the body of the North Vietnamese officer before Luke arrives to rescue him from permanently lapsing into violent insanity. Although Frank attempts to stop Ben his efforts are in vain. Ringo is already dead. During the fight, flames from burning oil drums form a significant part of the *mise-en-scene*. These fiery emblems anticipate an even greater inferno-esque world of corruption and violence awaiting them. Unlike the credit sequence, this fight ends in a deadlier manner.

Ben and Frank knock on Paul's door asking for help. Paul sees this as an opportunity to accomplish his dreams of material wealth. He arranges their departure from Hong Kong as couriers for Mr. Shing's activities by smuggling penicillin designed for Vietnam's black market. Ben and Frank have few options. They face arrest by the police for Ringo's murder, the vengeance of Ringo's gang, and demands by angry loan shark Kwai for repayment. All three hide in an abandoned World War II air raid shelter until Fatty (Lau Sek-yin) informs them of a planned escape route. During this scene, Paul appears isolated from Ben and Frank. He also looks into a fire. Its color evokes several ominous meanings. It not only heralds an apocalyptic journey into hell for all three but also visually intimates early stages of Paul's personal corruption. Shing shows the young men a photo of himself and his Saigon Chinatown counterpart Y. S. Leong (Lam Chung). The photograph represents another of Woo's ominous foreshadowing devices. Luke twice uses a photograph that Leong supplies him to identify his victims. Shing's presence in this photograph ironically suggests that he also may be another future victim of Leong's favorite method of disposing of business partners and rival gang members in his own organization. (Luke's second victim is the gangster who beats up Sally and sleeps with her). The final scene shows the trio at night overlooking a Hong Kong bay they may not see again for some time (Still 8). Paul stands slightly apart from the other two who are grouped closely together.

Still 8   The trio begins to separate.

The three young men are now at a turning point of their lives. Following the shot of Ringo's blood-spattered body on the ground, Woo uses an old-fashioned classical Hollywood wipe editing technique. Usually it represents a technical means to continue the film without slowing the narrative by showing irrelevant actions. But here it is much more significant. This first wipe to the right shows Ben and Frank knocking on Paul's door for help. Their actions unknowingly introduce a more destructive force into their lives. Paul sees the recent tragedy less in terms of helping his friends but more as an opportunity for making money to advance his career. In the Mandarin version of the film, Frank apologizes to Ben. "I really got you screwed, you and Jane." Ben replies, "We owe you so much." Another wipe reveals Jane waiting alone for Ben. She looks at an alarm clock. The clock ironically foreshadows their final separation during the Maoist demonstration sequence visualized by the ticking clock inside a deadly bomb. After the police (led by John Woo in a cameo role) knock on Jane's door enquiring for Ben, the sequence ends with a freeze frame close-up of Jane.[9] It then dissolves to a close-up of Ben seen in sharp focus to the right of the frame while Frank appears in soft focus on the left. The image then rack focuses to show Frank's face in sharp focus looking at his friend with concern. Frank occupies Jane's position in the preceding shot. The lap dissolve links Ben's new wife and trusted friend concerned for a man they both love in different ways. Woo supplies no explanation for Frank's look leaving it for audiences to supply their own conclusions. Frank's look may have homoerotic connotations. But deep friendship between men has always been a key component of *wuxia* literature and film. Frank knows that Ben thinks of Jane. The rack focus device has two related meanings. Frank's expression may not only reflect the concern he has for his friend and his sense of responsibility for separating him from Jane but also his recognition of Ben's violent side and fears concerning what their new criminal status may involve. Frank knows his friend very well.

After the night scene of the trio looking at Hong Kong's bay area, Woo cuts to another freeze frame he will activate to introduce a sequence rather than conclude it as in the final image of Ben's wedding. It begins with a freeze frame shot of Mao's Little Red Book held up by local Cultural Revolution activists demanding their own version of the colony's return to the Mainland: "Down with British Hong Kong." This time the demonstration is more serious than the earlier one outside Jane's factory. Hong Kong police again intervene but now in a more violent manner. They ferociously club not only Maoist demonstrators but also arrest innocent people such as one of Jane's female friends. Violence escalates during each demonstration in *Bullet in the Head* on the part of official authorities whether in Hong Kong or Saigon. Although Woo later sympathizes with the peaceful protest of the Buddhist monks in Saigon, he also recognizes that violent forces may use such situations for their own ends, making the situation much worse whether it be Hong Kong Maoists who use bombs or Viet Cong assassins using similar devices. Rapid explosions dominate this sequence. Fiery imagery again evokes Ben's attack on Ringo where flames rose from garbage cans. As Ben rescues Jane from the chaotic situation, the police discover an ominous package left next to a paper animal bearing the warning sign, "Urgent Order. Compatriots Stay Away." A bomb disposal expert arrives to dismantle the bomb as a clock ticks away. Woo intercuts these scenes with Ben's farewell to Jane in an intensively paced manner. Ben promises to return and take Jane away. His idealism evokes that earlier scene where he proposed to Jane and mimicked the motion of a bird flying away freely. Jane is more realistic. "The whole world is in turmoil. Who knows what tomorrow will bring." They kiss for the last time. Unlike Orson Welles's *Touch of Evil* (1958), a kiss does not immediately evoke an explosion.[10] Woo, instead, cuts to the clock inside the package opened by the bomb disposal officer, shows Jane moving away from Ben, and *then* shows the explosion, before revealing the agonized body of the young British bomb disposal expert whose armless right portion of the body occupies the entire frame.

Bullet in the Head contains many dualities where repetition frequently occurs in darker and more violent forms. The young officer loses his right arm. It is difficult to discern whether his other arm is also missing. Luke later loses his right arm when attempting to rescue the trio from the Viet Cong prison camp. *Bullet* does contain touching elements of romanticism. But Woo understands that this particular historical era and its violent eruptions contradict naïve utopian desires for escape. Although Ben and Jane kiss, any possibilities existing for individual salvation and romantic union become abruptly destroyed by apocalyptic violence. Woo symbolically merges the violence of the past (the Hong Kong riots of 1967) with forebodings of what the 1997 reunion with Mainland China may involve especially in the light of the Tiananmen Square massacre. This particular incident of apocalyptic violence involves the separation of lovers, families, and friends in the same way that the events of 1949, the Cultural Revolution, and the rush towards immigration from 1984 to 1997 entailed.[11] Woo left Hong Kong in 1992 and acquired American citizenship. Director Clara Law moved to Australia. Others such as Jackie Chan hedged their bets and decided not to take a chance by hasty emigration. Again, the fact that the 1997 reunion ended in a "whimper" and not an apocalyptic "bang" should not lead us to dismiss those serious forebodings existing at the time of the film's production. Another symbolic "future perfect" enactment also occurs in the Saigon demonstration sequences which explicitly incorporates Tiananmen Square into the narrative. Ben and Jane leave each other at a time of political turmoil. Their separation contains melodramatic, rather than romantic, overtones emphasizing that genre's employment of emotional and personal agony. Apocalyptic forces prevent the union of two people and lead to what may be their final separation. The last shot of this sequence is a close-up of Jane. Then the image fades to black as the curtain closes on this first act only to rise and reveal further apocalyptic threats in the following acts.

Part Two: The Saigon Apocalypse

Act Two opens with the three youngsters on a boat at dawn approaching Saigon. When they disembark with the smuggled penicillin destined for Mr. Leong, Paul cynically describes their situation. He caustically dismisses the plight of the Vietnamese. "Who gives a shit? It's their problem. Vietnamese killing Vietnamese. Nothing to do with us. We've come here to get rich." Paul reveals himself to be the archetypal Hong Kong capitalist out to make a quick buck. Stephen Chow Sing-chi's contemporary Cantonese comedies satirize such obnoxious character types. But Paul's attitude is more disturbing since it has deep roots within colony culture. As well as embodying Woo's fears about the loss of traditional humanitarian values in Hong Kong society, Paul's attitudes are not without historical precedent. Cai Chusheng's *Ten Thousand Li Ahead* (1941) depicts Hong Kong society as coarse and unforgiving. Mainland refugees fleeing from the Japanese discover that many Hong Kong citizens are "materialistic and indifferent to their plight as well as to the Sino-Japanese War effort on the Mainland."[12] The film's working-class heroes later discover that their employers are shipping merchandise to the Japanese. They then decide to leave Hong Kong and return to China to fight the enemy. Three decades later Tang Shuxuan's *China Behind* (1974) depicts the plight of Mainland refugees but this time they are five intellectuals seeking escape from the Cultural Revolution. Once they reach Hong Kong they find that they have exchanged one type of hell for another. Tang concludes her film in a devastating manner depicting the colony's inhumane materialism in several scenes that speak for themselves without need for commentary or explicit dialogue. Paul is not an isolated case. He shares many of Hong Kong's worst materialist values.

Inside a taxi, the three young men see a Saigon affected by the Vietnam War. Their perceptions indicate the different nature of their characters. Paul shows no interest in the city. He merely wishes to get the smuggled penicillin to Mr. Leong. Even at this early stage betrayal is on his mind as his previous lines show. "We can get more in Thailand." He wishes to buy a Mercedes with his first million, fulfilling a desire he earlier mentioned in Hong Kong.

Conscious of his separation from Jane, Ben looks at a G.I. with his Vietnamese wife and child. Frank dreams of buying embroidered slippers for his mother to replace the clogs she uses to beat him on the head. Although they all feel secure apocalyptic violence will again intervene, changing their lives more drastically than before.

Recreated in Thailand, the Saigon square prominently displays two film posters. One features Richard Harrison, a prolific American actor who appeared in many contemporary international productions such as Italian Westerns, European spy films cashing in on the James Bond phenomenon, and Hong Kong films such as Zhang Che's *Marco Polo* (1975) and *The Bloody Avengers* (1976). Woo may have known the actor's associations with his former mentor but he uses a period poster from one of Harrison's Italian films, *Duello nel Mondo*, also known as *Duel dans le Monde* and *Ring Around the World*. Co-directed by Georges Combret and Luigi Scattini, the film featured Harrison as an American detective traveling around the globe to solve an insurance mystery. The poster ironically evokes the trio's relocation to a more nearby destination where they will not be masters of their individual destinies like Hollywood heroes of international co-productions. As the original Italian and French titles suggest, another ominous duel will occur later between Ben and Paul in the dark urban environment of Hong Kong. Another film poster appears in the Vietnamese *Tu Saigon den Dien Bien Phu*. Although commentators such as Bey Logan suggest that Woo refers to Pierre Schoendoerffer's *Dien Bien Phu* (1991), which was currently being shot on location in Vietnam at the same time as *Bullet in the Head*, the reference may actually be a fictional parallel to earlier Indochina Western co-production films such as David Butler's *Jump into Hell* (1955). Starring Jacques Sernas, Kurt Kasznar, and Peter Van Eyck, *Jump into Hell* dealt with the last days of French colonial rule. Made a year after French involvement in Vietnam, the film presented a one-sided Cold War version of historical events. Although *Jump into Hell* is black and white, color films did not dominate Southeast Asia screens until much later. Hong Kong productions such as Zhang Che's *Tiger Boy* (1965) and Lung Gong's *Story of a Discharged Prisoner* (1967, which influenced John Woo's *A Better Tomorrow*), and virtually every North Vietnam film shot during the actual period of the war were all black and white productions.[13] From a political perspective, *Jump into Hell* was a much safer film to show in South Vietnam at the time rather than Schoendoerffer's more devastating *The 317th Platoon* (1964) that foreshadowed the eventual victory of the North Vietnamese in 1975. Although he does not wear the head covering in the poster of *Jump into Hell*, the image strongly resembles an Eastern version of Jacques Sernas who, unlike Schoendoerffer's French characters in *The 317th Platoon* and *Dien Bien Phu*, does escape at the end.

As the taxi containing the smuggled penicillin makes its way through Saigon, an abrupt cut reveals a shoeshine boy eagerly cleaning the boots of an unseen military officer. He smiles at his customer in an archetypal colonial manner of a subject race playing up to Western stereotypical imagery. At the same moment a South Vietnamese general enters his car. The authorities halt the traffic for this V.I.P. During the following scenes Woo again consolidates his reputation as one of Hong Kong's most accomplished directors of action sequences. But moral consequences are not absent. Their presence challenges those audience members who merely wish to gratuitously indulge in watching violent spectacles. The later execution scenes in the Viet Cong prison camp similarly question any non-complicated pleasures on the part of audiences who attempt avoiding serious implications behind Woo's manner of representing violence.

A Viet Cong suicide attack begins as a motorcyclist rides towards the general's car. His aides advise him to crouch down rather than leave the vehicle and seek safety elsewhere. By contrast, the taxi driver urges Ben, Frank, and Paul to leave the car. Instead of immediately taking the taxi driver's advice, Paul attempts to loosen the straps binding the suitcase carrying the penicillin from the top of the taxi. But his friends drag him away. Paul prefers money over human life — even his own. The military shoot the motorcyclist. He crashes into the taxi and explodes it. This leads to the second part of the assassination plan. The shoeshine boy now moves into action. He sets off a bomb inside his box, runs to the general's car, and throws it inside. As the bomb explodes, Ben, Frank, and Paul fall over him. They ironically protect the assassin from the effects of the explosion he caused. However, their humanitarian act is futile. The Saigon military immediately round up every suspect and rush them into the compound of a Catholic school run by nuns.

Prior to this roundup, Woo presents the Catholic school as a peaceful sanctuary in a violent world. He borrows from the North Vietnamese school sequence in Francis Ford Coppola's *Apocalypse Now* (1979) where the arrival of American helicopters at the beginning of the "Ride of the Valkyries" sequence violently destroys a peaceful community. Like those Budddhist monks later seen at the beginning of the Saigon demonstration, the nuns represent marginalized peaceful values threatened by outside forces of historical and political apocalyptic violence. Like the female North Vietnamese school teacher in Coppola's film, the nuns move their children away from approaching chaos. Unlike Coppola's "Ride of the Valkyries," which brought his film to a climactic high point during its middle part, Woo's particular sequence is no device of spectacular showmanship having no intrinsic relationship to the rest of the narrative. Instead it unleashes a devastating chain of destructive circumstances that will last until the final shot of *Bullet in the Head*.

Once inside the schoolyard, a brutal ARVN officer (Army of the Republic of Vietnam) begins his interrogation. The military close the school gates to prevent reporters (including many Western press representatives and one based on photojournalist Eddie Adams) from viewing the brutal type of interrogation that America allows its allies to conduct. *Bullet in the Head* belongs to a time when investigative journalism could freely expose the hideous world of American foreign policy free from today's restrictions. Woo chooses to reproduce the ugly incident of the murder of Viet Cong suspect Bei Lop during the Tet Offensive in 1968 in this sequence. His brief shots of photojournalists outside the school gates intuitively evoke another reference: police brutality during the 1968 Democratic Convention in Chicago when battered demonstrators chanted "The Whole World is Watching" as photographers captured the real meaning of American democracy for the rest of the world. Woo wants audiences to watch and understand the ugly nature of a violent world encompassing past, present, and future.

Awaiting interrogation by the ARVN, Paul reaches his breaking point. "I won't let them shoot me." By contrast, Frank attempts to comfort somebody he believes is his friend. He reassures Paul, "It's all right. We're not local." Despite this, Paul waves his passport pleading, "I'm Hong Kong people." British passport and different nationality make no impression. The incident represents an ironic future perfect reference to a nightmare situation two decades later. Then Prime Minister Margaret Thatcher disregarded British citizenship claims of Hong Kong residents in the same way as those of the Falkland Island inhabitants in 1982 by devaluing the status of their passports. The scene also uncannily anticipates the current practices of the CIA and Homeland Security in today's "War on Terror." When Ben, Frank, and Paul attempt to assert their Hong Kong identity before a different military power that dismisses their claims, the incident would evoke dark feelings on the part of Hong Kong residents watching the Tiananmen Square incident. They would fear similar treatment by the People's Liberation Army in 1997.

Vietnam also had a large Chinese community. Ben also states that "We're Chinese, Hong Kong people." He wishes to assert a different identity than Mainland Chinese nationality and vainly appeals to Vietnamese knowledge of another type of Chinese community having nothing in common with Mainland support of Ho Chi Minh. Before the trio experience further violence, the ARVN discover the real bomber. When he jeers and spits at an officer, a pistol is drawn and placed to his head. The nuns now withdraw their children away from looking at the imminent scene of deadly violence. Outside the gates the press cry, "We want to take pictures. We have the right to know."

One photographer will take a picture that later influenced Woo's recreation: Eddie Adams. His picture circulated throughout the world. But Woo chooses to depict this well-documented incident in his own creative manner. When the officer shoots the suspect through the head, Woo films this violent act in slow motion. As the suspect's body falls below the frame, Woo uses rack focus to put into sharp perspective a background image: a Pieta statue of Mary, mother of Jesus, embracing the dead body of her son taken down from the Cross (Still 9). This reference is multi-dimensional. Woo does not intend to equate the murdered suspect with the Savior. He regards North and South Vietnamese as equal sides of the same murderous coin violently engaging in a contemporary currency of historical and political violence. Both political opponents utilize criminal enterprises designed to make money. The murdered suspect is no savior since he has committed murder. Instead, Woo's Pieta imagery represents another of his brief, but significant, symbolic references to a spiritual realm offering alternatives to human violence that few choose to follow. The ARVN officer's act of murder is no different from the one performed by his victim. These incidents represent further examples of that fallen world the Savior originally took on human form to redeem without any humanitarian and permanent results for his effort being present two millennia later. His goal of salvation still awaits fulfillment. Despite his Christian sympathies, Woo is also conscious of this fact and engages in no false optimism.

Still 9   Death of a Viet Cong martyr.

Woo emphasizes the particular nature of a murder crucial to the future development of *Bullet in the Head*. It is the first actual bullet in the head that occurs in the film. Frank's earlier bloody head wounds at the end of Ben's wedding anticipated this ugly event. The murder sequence displays a moment of apocalyptic violence that will symbolically echo throughout the rest of the film like the sound of a bullet leaving its deadly chamber remaining to haunt the key players of this drama. When Ben later ends Frank's psychological and spiritual torment in the mean streets of Saigon, the concluding slow-motion image reveals Frank lifting a gun into the right lower frame. It complements the earlier scene when the Viet Cong suspect's head moved below the left frame following his death against the Pieta in the background towards the right of the frame. A bullet in the head will occur again on two other deadly occasions. This first occurrence sets off a deadly chain of events leading to an apocalyptic chain reaction as tragic as those in any Greek play or Jacobean melodrama.

The Bolero Club Inferno

The murder leaves its mark on the three fugitives. They go to the edge of a Saigon river. Traumatically affected by what he has seen, Frank throws up while Ben and Paul stand by his side. Woo cuts to an overhead shot as he looks down on the three, noting their individual positions (Still 10). Frank kneels over. His position recalls his vulnerable one during the end of the chicken-run sequence in Hong Kong. But now, the stakes are different. As in the earlier night sequence when they looked over Kowloon Bay before their departure for Vietnam, Ben stands nearest to Frank. But Paul now stands further away from them. Woo then records the different reactions of Ben and Paul. He zooms in to Paul showing his studied reaction to the murder they have all recently witnessed. Paul obviously decides to learn from this display of powerful violence. By contrast, Woo dollies round Ben suggesting a more ambiguous attitude of someone who remains undecided as to which path he will follow. Paul then states, "With a gun in our hands, there's no going back. The whole world will be ours." His final sentence anticipates his first appearance in Act Four where he revolves a globe in his office before going to a meeting where he will take over from his retiring boss Mr. Kwan. Woo concludes this sequence cutting to individual close-ups of Frank and Ben. Their faces express concern for Paul and the direction he is moving towards.

Still 10   Violence further separates three friends.

The next scene begins with the trio outside Leong's Bolero Club. It is an environment illustrating further apocalyptic violence. When inside, they see an appropriately red-colored hellish environment devoted to making money. Mid close-ups of currency thrust into female dancers' stocking tops by American G.I.s emphasize this. Ironically, a 60s rock group plays the familiar theme of "I'm a Believer" heard in the beginning of the film. This theme formerly contrasted two opposing realms: the church hall where Ben directed his young students within a utopian world of dance and an outside violent environment dominated by Ringo. "I'm a Believer" now becomes more closely identified with the violence depicted in the second credit sequence with Leong functioning as an older version of Ringo who has risen in the Triad hierarchy in the same way as Paul hopes to do. The Bolero Club is a world of material gain and violence welcoming those who want to join and become believers in its value system. Paul's perverse "Pilgrim's Progress" will lead him to make this choice. The Bolero Club's "satanic majesty," Y. S. Leong, deals with whatever side gives him the most money, whether North or South, and punishes anyone who desires his property, whether human (Sally) or material.

Leong enters the crowded interior Bolero Club accompanied by his entourage. He resembles a gangster from any classical Hollywood or Triad movie. His presence impresses Paul. "Look. There's Mr. Leong. You can tell he's a big shot." (The Mandarin dialogue version of the film translates Paul's remark to Frank as "You should take Mr. Leong as an example. His nose is in the air.") Paul admires Leong from a distance as he walks into the club with others in the manner of a royal procession. Ben and Frank do not share Paul's fascination. Instead, they see a well-known Hong Kong celebrity: Sally (Yolinda Yan Choh-sin). They recognize her as a local Hong Kong Cantopop singer but note the change in her appearance as a result of her drug dependency and forced prostitution. Apart from her later Saigon meeting with Ben during daylight where she wears a white Vietnamese *ao dai* costume, Sally wears red throughout the film, a color denoting less of a "fallen woman" status according to Western standards but evoking the color of Jane's traditional bridal outfit in the wedding sequence. Some critics see Yolinda Yan's performance as another example of Woo's inability to develop female characters. But Yan's passive performance may be intentional. After humiliating drug dependency and white slavery by an abusive employer, who has hired her not only for her singing qualities, Sally suffers from emotional numbness. Drugs take their toll on her and she remains disappointed by the failure of a male savior, representing traditional *wuxia* values, to rescue her from personal degradation. Sally is the "damsel in distress" of *Bullet in the Head*. But Woo realizes that there can be no Hollywood "happy ending" for another victim of this fallen world.

Still 11   The arrival of Luke.

One "knight" has already failed her: Luke (Still 11). In his only film to date with John Woo, Simon Yam Tat-wah receives a classical Hollywood star entrance. Introduced by the French tune *Autumn Leaves*, Yam's Eurasian hit-man represents Woo's new version of

Chow Yun-fat's "noble" character from *The Killer* derived from Alain Delon's assassin in Jean Pierre Melville's *Le Samourai* (1965). Patrick Leong confirms in his DVD feature interview that Luke's white suit deliberately parallels that worn by the title character of *The Killer*.[14] Like deadly silent assassin Chong (Lung Ming-yan) in *A Better Tomorrow 2*, Luke has his own code of honor. But he is trapped by a world of corruption. As Bey Logan frequently points out in his audio-commentary to the British DVD release of *Bullet in the Head*, Luke appears outwardly perfect but inwardly scarred. After saving Frank, he achieves redemption through sacrifice in a manner reversing the nature of his first appearance. He becomes outwardly scarred but inwardly perfect. Jeff in *The Killer* dies following his final attempt to rescue Jenny (Sally Yeh Chian-wen) after the gunfight in the church. Luke lives on. Like the bomb disposal officer in Hong Kong, he loses his right arm, making any attempt to resume his former profession totally impossible. But he will never want to return to it again. He becomes at peace with himself and decides to remain in South Vietnam. As an anonymous reviewer has suggested, this may be another connection to Woo's mentor Zhang Che whose one-armed swordsman wishes to leave his former profession at the end of *One Armed Swordsman* and *Return of the One-Armed Swordsman* (1969).

When we first see Luke, he greets a French pianist in the Bolero giving him a cigar as a silent code to obtain a hidden gun to carry out his next assignment for Leong. Like hired assassin Chong in *A Better Tomorrow 2*, he performs this act with calculated efficiency. Luke embodies Woo's version of those old knightly figures of the *wuxia* tradition now facing a different world like Jeff and Chong. Resembling unemployed *ronin*, they have fallen from grace and become reduced to the humiliating position of putting their talents at the service of new masters far inferior to those Chinese *sifu*s and Japanese *samurai* lords who used them for more prestigious tasks. These killers now exist within their twentieth-century types of limbo and purgatory, waiting for the moment when they can redeem themselves even if it means personal annihilation. Woo uses a red filter to introduce Luke as he obtains his weapon from the pianist. It appropriately symbolizes the hellish way this damned soul now uses his talents. Although a secondary character in *Bullet in the Head*, Luke parallels characters in Woo's other films. In *A Better Tomorrow 2*, Chong ignores the advice of his boss to take the money and run when the odds turn against them. This impassive figure with white gloves and dark glasses, evoking Alain Delon's "samourai" in the full Japanese sense of the word, contemptuously looks at the money placed before him on a table before slowly departing to fight Ken Gor (Chow Yun-fat). For Chong, the battle is a matter of honor, not to be contaminated by material values. This is one of the great moments in Woo's cinema where he affirms those traditional heroic values of the past dismissed by a new generation of bosses such as Shing (Waise Lee) in *A Better Tomorrow*, Ko (Kwan San) in *A Better Tomorrow 2*, Johnny Weng (Shing Fui-on) in *The Killer*, Leong, Johnny Wong (Anthony Wong Chau-sang) in *Hard Boiled*, and Paul in the concluding act of *Bullet in the Head*.

In *Hard Boiled*, "Mad Dog" (played by veteran Shaw Brothers actor and action director Philip Kwok Chun-fung) finally rejects Johnny Wong's dishonorable actions and is shot for attempting to stop bloodshed going beyond the acceptable moral boundaries of his hideous profession.[15] Later in *Bullet in the Head*, Luke enters Leong's safe. He briefly looks at the strong box containing the gold leaf (desired by Paul) and the hidden C.I.A. plans. Then he, nonchalantly, closes the lid showing no interest in money. Luke prefers to help his new-found friends take Sally away from Leong who only views her as a money-making commodity.

Frank recognizes Sally from their Hong Kong days. Now reduced to servitude by Leong, she rejects the advances of one of his customers only to receive the comment, "I'm sure you are used to being touched by strangers." Leong's enigmatic remark receives full explanation later during Sally's flashback account of her past to Ben. But Woo also intuitively supplies the answer in one of his inimitable camera movements. After Luke sits down in the Bolero waiting to carry out an assassination, the camera slowly dollies round him from right to left as he looks forward. This follows a shot of Sally looking at him. Luke appears fully aware of the danger he will put her in if he looks back at her. Woo frames this camera movement with shots of Sally looking at him as if pleading for some form of recognition. However, Luke knows from past experience what will happen. A later flashback explains why he ignores her. After running away from Leong's table, she stumbles before Ben who intuitively recognizes someone who needs help. Luke and Leong observe this action in separate shots. These images again reveal Woo's carefully structured editing within a film where no shot is ever accidental. Ben's concern for Sally evokes Luke's earlier heroic attempt to help her. The observant Leong sees another version of this earlier event about to begin (Still 12). Sally asks why Ben should want to help her. He answers, "Because we are Chinese" in the subtitles but Tony Leung's actual dialogue mentions their Hong Kong origins.

Still 12   The deadly Mr. Leong.

Luke introduces himself to Frank and Paul but then excuses himself to perform his next deadly mission for Leong who has set up a greedy customs official for assassination (Still 13). This occurs in the restroom where Ben and Luke meet each other for the first time. Although Woo playfully brings overtones of a gay pick-up into this scene, the implications are more serious and Woo achieves this in the best manner of silent cinema without any need for dialogue. The scene opens with Ben in center foreground close-up washing his hands. Luke enters in the background. Ben turns to see him. Luke's face appears in close-up. It is almost as if he intuitively recognizes a fellow fallen knight in a hellish twentieth-century world that has no noble use for their talents. He gestures with his eyes for Ben to move away. Ben immediately gets the message and removes himself from the line of fire allowing Luke to carry out his assassination by shooting his victim who falls into the urinal in a similar motion to one of Colonel Everett Dasher-Breed's military thugs in *The Dirty Dozen* (1967). His mission accomplished, Luke looks once again at Ben via a close-up shot then leaves. Throughout this sequence Woo employs his third and most violent use of "I'm a Believer." Here it accompanies an act of assassination where the victim has no chance of defending himself

Still 13   Mr. Leong jokes with his intended victim.

unlike the earlier Rumble sequence. The stakes are much higher here. To become a "Believer" means recognizing that the world is a violent place. But this does not mean total submission to any idea that ends justify means, a conclusion Paul follows. The world is a violent place. Some people *believe* that. But others such as Ben and Luke also intuitively *believe* in peaceful alternatives although they find themselves in a world forcing them to perform actions violating their better selves. John Woo, the Buddhist monks, and those Catholic schoolteachers of *Bullet in the Head*, who exist on the margins of a violent society, form another alternative. Ben and Luke are trapped in a hellish environment recognizing themselves as kindred spirits who have no way out at this point of the film.

After Luke leaves the restroom, one of Leong's men hands him a roll of money. He takes the bundle without even looking at it, exhibiting the same type of attitude as Chong in *A Better Tomorrow 2*. Outside the Bolero, Frank and Paul introduce Luke to Ben. Neither of them mentions the ugly circumstances surrounding their previous meeting. Woo next introduces Luke's apartment by displaying three items: a poster of Catherine Deneuve (subtly stressing his Eurasian origins), a model of a Chinese junk (whose significance will soon be revealed in Sally's flashback), and a record player with "Autumn Leaves" playing. The song has a special significance in the film since it suggests a pessimistic romanticism applying not only to the love affair between Luke and Sally but also intimating how it will end. Paul immediately plans to cheat Leong since they have lost the penicillin. He asks Luke's advice about guns. "I won't sweep the streets like my Dad ... In this world, if you have a gun, you have everything." Luke reluctantly agrees to help him. Ben and Frank again note the changes in their friend. As Paul gazes at a gun in fascination after saying, "Tell me, how much does a human life cost?", Woo inserts one of his significant shots. Ben first appears in soft focus in the background while Paul is in sharp focus. Woo then racks the focus to show Ben's image to sharp focus revealing his concerned look at the change in his friend's attitude. The image recalls that earlier scene of Ben and Frank looking with concern at Paul after witnessing the murder of the Viet Cong suspect. Luke will take Paul's place with Woo offering one damned soul the possibility of salvation rather than a former friend who appears about to say, "Evil. Be thou my good." For those viewers attentive to Waise Lee's performance up to this point of the film, this change is not accidental. Paul has only waited for the right time to display his real character.

Like James Cagney's Tom Powers in *Public Enemy* (1931), Paul acquires his first gun. He now wishes to see how powerful the weapon will make him. The following day, to Frank's amazement, Paul refuses to pay for an over-priced soft drink at a Saigon store and pulls a gun on the owner demanding money. Despite this act, Frank protects his friend by firing a warning shot at a security guard rather than shooting to kill. Paul expresses amazement at his first financial success. "Look, it was such an easy job. He was scared to death." The two "Hongkies" run off with their loot only to encounter an ARVN jeep stopping before the Kim Thanh jewelry store. Like the deadly fight against Ringo in Hong Kong, individual events in this closely edited action sequence are significant. Frank and Paul soon understand that the guns pointing at them do not mean their arrest. After several attempts verbally telling them to "get down" in Vietnamese, an ARVN soldier finally gives them the message in sign language by lowering his machine gun. They fall down beside the loot Paul has taken from the store. After shooting the owners of this Korean-Vietnamese business, the soldiers go on a looting expedition emphasized by close-ups of hands grabbing jewelry. Woo's original cut repeated these close-ups, warning his audiences again about the violent associations of material values. Significantly, a GOLD STAR sign appears inside the jeweler's shop. It anticipates the "gold leaf" bullion that will finally cast its spell on Paul. As the jeep moves away, Paul now receives his third lesson involving the violent power of weapons, the first being the execution of the Viet Cong suspect and the second his easy robbery at the Vietnamese store. He will later reject friendship for gold using weaponry to achieve his ends. The sequence ironically concludes with Paul picking up the Vietnamese currency he and Frank threw to the ground when they thought the ARVN were about to arrest them.

Ben proceeds to his agreed rendezvous at Bak Lop Bridge with Sally. But, as in the previous Hong Kong sequence depicting his farewell to Jane, he encounters another world of political violence. Buddhist monks lead a peaceful anti-war demonstration. While one subtitled DVD version of *Bullet in the Head* translates Buddhist demands as "We want the governor to respect our peaceful desires," various banner signs contain logos such as US MUST WITHDRAW FROM SOUTH VIETNAM and UNIFY SOUTH VIETNAM. These pleas conflate two levels of historical reality: the actual 1968 situation in South Vietnam when the American presence received devastating assault and Hong Kong at the time of the film's production as seen in the reference to "governor" rather than the president who ruled South Vietnam in 1968. Woo again conflates different historical and political events when he refers to another well-known contemporary historical image: that famous shot of the lone protestor demonstrating against a People's Liberation Army tank in Tiananmen Square in 1989. It parallels his earlier appropriation of the famous Eddie Adams photo. This is another example of Woo creatively reworking certain features within David Lean historical epics such as *The Bridge on the River Kwai* (1957), *Lawrence of Arabia* (1962), *Dr. Zhivago* (1967), and *Ryan's Daughter* (1970) where individuals find themselves caught up within turbulent political forces they find themselves powerless to oppose.

Ben and Sally find themselves briefly separated by the demonstration. The ARVN uses violence against the peaceful protestors and are far more vicious than the Hong Kong police, shooting into the crowd as well as clubbing individuals on the head.

These acts involve excessive violence on the part of another establishment against those who dare question its rule. Grim fears of Tiananmen Square and forebodings of what 1997 may really involve dominate these scenes. Woo uses his own type of Eisenstein montage involving key elements of emotional and political meaning by merging scenes of the Hong Kong Maoist demonstration, Ben's last moments with Jane, the bomb explosion, with his rescue of Sally. She stumbles in the crowd in the same way as Jane did in 1967 Hong Kong. Using brief flashback imagery, Woo repeats Jane's lines to Ben. "Forget it. Everywhere is the same." No escape appears possible from powerful historical forces of apocalyptic political violence that threaten everyone trapped within their domain.

Most theatrical and DVD versions of *Bullet in the Head* show Woo's brave Tiananmen Square demonstrator being brutally led away by the ARVN (Still 14). It represents one contemporary version of what might have actually happened although another story mentions that the crowd dragged him to safety. Several scenes were removed from this sequence revealing that Woo developed its dark implications even further as surviving fragments suggest. One shot shows the ARVN brutally beating the demonstrator on the head making it as bloody as Frank's wound by Ringo before they drag

Still 14   The recent memory of Tiananmen Square.

him away. Blood copiously flows from his head. Woo's "bullet in the head" metaphor now becomes collective rather than individual. Other missing scenes emphasized Ben watching the demonstration paralleling the 1989 situation of Hong Kong citizens looking at the events of Tiananamen Square on their television sets, extra footage of demonstrators, the presence of a photographer (who like Eddie Adams in 1968 would capture another historically significant scene), more shots of the U.S. embassy gates that remain closed to Vietnamese seeking refuge as they would later do in 1975, extra footage of Ben rushing to help Sally, and more shots of him embracing Sally as he did Jane during their final parting in Hong Kong.[16]

The Rescue of Sally

The next scene shows Ben and Sally meeting at their agreed rendezvous by a wharf overlooking the sea. As Bey Logan points out in his audio-commentary, the River Kwai in Thailand substitutes for the Bak Lop Bridge. One wonders whether this location represents another reference to a David Lean film, *The Bridge on the River Kwai*. Sally is a prisoner of Leong who has forced her into drug addiction and prostitution after stealing her Hong Kong British passport. When Ben asks whether anybody attempted to help her, Woo employs a flashback within a flashback introducing Luke as her unlikely knight errant. After Luke murders Leong's thug who beat her up in the first part of her own flashback depicting brutalization at the hands of her new master, Sally appeals to the assassin for help. She tells Ben of how they often sat on the very same place they inhabit now and dreamed of escaping by boat until Leong intervened one day. Ben assures her that they will all escape by the same route. "We came here by boat. We'll return home the same way." As Kevin Heffernan points out, this explains the presence of the Chinese junk model in Luke's house.[17]

Scene five of this second act opens with Luke and his three allies united in a plan to rescue Sally. Some missing footage probably explained how they agreed to this as well as the mysterious manner as to how Leong found out — unless we are to assume he obtained the information when Sally was high on drugs. The three Hongkies arrive outside the Bolero Club. Paul wears a suit and tie deliberately imitating the style of the big timer he intends to "rip off" while Ben and Frank wear casual attire with open necked shirts. Luke enters offering his pianist contact a cigar at the very moment one of Leong's henchmen descends the stairs before frisking him for weapons. Mistaking Luke's collection of cigars for the real thing he allows him upstairs oblivious of the fact that they are really explosive devices. Luke introduces the three men to Leong as colleagues of his Hong Kong associate Shing there to deliver a suitcase supposedly containing penicillin. Prior to their arrival, Leong completed a deal with ARVN officers involving gold leaf bullion and C.I.A. documents to sell to the North Vietnamese. This possibly explains why he does not examine the suitcase. He is less concerned with "small fry" smuggling at this point. Instead, he plans his own sadistic type of revenge against Ben who he sees as a threat to his acquisition of Sally. The big timer plans to "entertain" them downstairs. While they wait for Leong, Frank expresses apprehension. "I hope nobody gets killed." Paul ominously replies, "I'll kill anyone who gets in my way."

Many critics acclaim the Bolero Club massacre as a major example of Woo's action film expertise. But its dynamic nature is merely the tip of a creative iceberg. Here Woo meticulously examines conflicting tensions affecting a noble cause in this sequence. Deeper levels of meaning co-exist in a film that deserves more detailed analysis rather than praise for its spectacular displays of bloodshed and weaponry. Jealous of Ben's concern for Sally, Leong begins to probe his victims. While Frank mentions that they knew Sally as a Cantopop singer in Hong Kong, Ben taunts the older man (to Paul's dismay) by commenting upon her unhappy demeanor. The angry Leong reveals his knowledge of their rescue plot. He begins his humiliation tactics by forcing Ben to consume a full bottle of whisky. Frank intervenes by snatching the bottle and helping his friend once again. "I made the screw up. I'll drink." He consumes the entire bottle while Sally looks on singing the number "Wildflowers/Dandelion" that Frank associated with her happier Hong Kong career. Leong's sadistic form of torment does not stop there. In a scene edited from most prints, he instructs his henchmen to urinate into beer glasses and makes his victims drink from them. At this point of the narrative, Sally cannot continue her number and leaves the stage. Ben takes up the challenge and drinks the full amount. So does Frank. Paul cannot and throws up to the amusement of Leong. Paul then expresses anger at Ben who responds, "I did that for all of us." Frank and Paul immediately stage a fight so they can retrieve weapons hidden in the piano to begin fighting against Leong and his men. After taking revenge by pouring urine from a beer glass on Leong's head, Ben forces him upstairs.[18]

While Luke earlier failed in saving Sally, Ben succeeds in rescuing her from two of Leong's thugs who have injected her with drugs. As in the Saigon robbery, Frank again helps Paul. But this time he shoots two of Leong's men rather than firing a warning shot. Frank now begins his own odyssey form of contamination by violence that will lead to ugly consequences. However, he also helps his best friend Ben once again by uniting him with Sally. His deed parallels his earlier gesture of friendship that enabled Ben to marry Jane. Ben reaffirms his promise to Sally despite the presence of an angry Paul who sees her presence as an obstacle to his plans. "Are you guys crazy? That's your business. Cut me out." Frank answers: "Stop it Paul. If we're still buddies, it doesn't matter." But it will. Frank looks at Ben and Sally. Again recognizing the value of his friend's devotion, Ben hands Sally over to Frank while he goes in search of her passport.

Ben and Luke now attempt to force Leong to reveal its location. Paul just wants to steal money and harangues Luke. "You said it was here. Where's the gold?" His frenzied question parallels Ethan Edward's obsessive one to Mose Harper in *The Searchers* (1956) about the location of Scar while the more humane Matthew wants to rescue Debbie. Guessing where Leong has concealed the passport, Luke goes to the safe and retrieves it. He casually opens the bullion box, looks briefly at its contents, and walks away. By contrast, when Paul goes to the safe he finds his heart's desire (Still 15). Woo shoots his face in a low-angle close-up lit up by the reflection of gold bullion suggesting demonic possession. This is the first of three similar shots that Woo uses to reveal to viewers that Paul is now a lost cause. He will no longer affirm bonds of friendship with Ben and Frank. Instead, Luke will take his place. Woo confirms this in one interesting shot sequence. It occurs prior to the group's effort to escape the Bolero Club with Leong as their hostage. Woo shows Luke looking in friendship at Ben confirming that intuitive feeling of blood brotherhood recognition when they first met in the restroom. He then cuts and zooms in to Ben. Woo also uses the same camera movement for Frank in the next shot. By contrast, Woo separates Paul from the other three men by cutting to a static shot of him as he primes his rifle. Monetary gain rather than Sally's rescue really motivates him.[19]

Still 15   The reflection of gold tempts Paul.

Luke forces Leong to undress so his clothes can be used for a henchmen decoy to distract the gang waiting outside. Although, it is a good strategy, it also represents poetic justice. Two flashbacks previously revealed Sally's humiliation in a state of undress by one of Leong's thugs and Leong himself. Leong now experiences a similar form of humiliation in a reverse situation where he is now the captive.

As well as being a feast of visual spectacle, the escape from the Bolero Club also contains other important features. Some of Paul's gold leaf bullion spills onto the floor. The box appears about to fall into the hands of Leong's men but Paul prevents this. His supposedly "heroic" actions are less noble than material. He shoots his assailants not to facilitate the group's escape but exclusively to retrieve his loot. Woo uses a second close-up of Paul's avaricious face illuminated by gold leaf now spilled on the floor as he challenges his adversaries. "Bastards! Don't touch *my* gold." He performs this action isolated from his associates in several shots.

Sally loses her passport during the escape. This allows Leong to snatch her away from Ben, attempting to use her as a hostage before shooting her in the back. As Leong tries to escape, Ben and Luke fire bullets into him. Several penetrate his legs. During the climactic Hong Kong confrontation between Ben and Paul, the evil member of the original trio also receives a bullet in *his* leg, emphasizing again parallels between Leong and Paul. While Luke and Paul exit the Bolero Club with Sally, Ben and Frank use Leong as a hostage for the last time. They now face Leong's corrupt ARVN associates and remaining gang members using Luke's explosive cigars to aid their escape. Were it left to Paul alone, he would abandon them. He urges Luke to drive away but Luke ignores his selfish demands.

The next scene forms an appropriate coda to preceding events. As the group drives away, they find themselves in the middle of a U.S. Army roadblock under attack by North Vietnamese forces.

Luke uses his C.I.A. background and American-accented English to get them through the chaotic landscape of a night disrupted by apocalyptic explosions, huge tanks, and military conflict. The sequence evokes Jane's parting words to Ben during the violent Maoist demonstration. "The whole world is in turmoil. Who knows what tomorrow will bring?" Driving through frightened crowds of refugees, Paul contemptuously remarks, "They're hopeless." But Frank begins giving them the Vietnamese money most of which is probably from Paul's earlier robbery. Frank passes some currency to Ben who also repeats his friend's humanitarian gesture. During this sequence, the main *Bullet in the Head* musical theme by James Wong and Romero Diaz plays prominently on the soundtrack. Formerly associated with those former carefree days of friendship in Hong Kong, it now takes on a more somber and resilient tone. It is somber since these young men are now in a very serious situation but it is also resilient since it demonstrates a will to survive overwhelming historical forces signified by the huge American tank (evoking the one in the Saigon/Tiananmen Square sequence) and the explosive forces of a violent deadly night threatening to overwhelm them. At the same time, the fugitives move deeper into Woo's personal and political apocalyptic heart of darkness.

Part Three: A Season in Hell

Act Three opens in daylight by a riverbank. Luke has arranged a rendezvous with a boat that will take them to safety. The Hong Kong friends move even further apart. A long shot reveals an isolated Paul standing beside his loot. He opens the box to gaze in fascination at the gold leaf. His face appears again in close-up illuminated by yellow light for the third time in the film. Agitated by the late arrival of their transport and displaying no concern for the dying Sally, Paul's selfish behavior evokes an angry response from Frank. It is the first of several during this sequence. "Are you human? Spare a thought for us. You only care for your gold." Frank's response represents what Woo has already revealed to us in three suggestive close-ups. The others finally recognize the change in his character. Paul becomes as dehumanized as one of Count Dracula's victims. Here the former victim of downward capitalist mobility now becomes a victimizer eager to use and abuse others for his own dark purposes.[20] When the boat arrives, Luke discerns some warning signs in a manner similar to Aaron Edwards's suspicions of an imminent Indian attack in *The Searchers*. He is not wrong. Leong's men and his ARVN associates appear. Another battle commences. While Ben, Frank, and Luke fight off the assailants, Paul ignores them. He rushes to the boat with his loot offering its captain money to help him aboard. However, greed receives its appropriate reward. The captain pays for ignoring his own personal safety and succumbing to monetary temptation by dying in a hail of bullets and falling into the water in Woo's homage to Sam Peckinpah's balletic, slow-motion, montage style seen in *The Wild Bunch* (1968).[21] Woo here emphasizes pain, suffering, and a particular moral message more than the gratuitous violence of Quentin Tarantino and his contemporaries.[22]

While Paul attempts to start the boat, the others rush to safety after Luke has left explosive devices to stall their adversaries. Although they appear to win on this occasion, Sally's death undermines this victory. Woo cuts to a close-up of her passport falling into the water at the moment of her passing. Ben persuades Luke to let her go. Her body floats in the water evoking that poignant moment of farewell to a dead comrade in *Apocalypse Now* in a scene Coppola borrowed from Budd Boetticher's *Ride Lonesome* (1959). The "*Apocalypse Now*" influence also becomes explicit. Woo uses a long shot of the boat traveling down the river similar to the one in Coppola's film showing Willard and Chef

approaching the heart of darkness. The young men from Hong Kong
will soon experience their own version of "the horror."

Ben, Frank, and Luke sit at the front of the boat in silence.
Paul gleefully pilots them towards a safe haven for his material
advantage.[23] However, his joy is short-lived. The engine breaks
down. He attempts in vain to get his companions to help. Paul
hypocritically tells them that he also mourns Sally's death but then
reveals his real feelings. "But it's better this way. She won't hold us
down." When he further displays his other motivations, "If this
boat sinks, we'll lose all the gold," Ben reacts against his selfish
behavior. He begins throwing the gold leaf into the river. Paul points
his gun at Ben's head leading Frank to protect Ben by pointing his
gun at Paul's own head (Still 16). This is Woo's familiar use of the
"Mexican Stand-Off." Borrowed and imitated by hack Hollywood
talents ever since, it seems to be a mere director's signature
equivalent to Alfred Hitchcock's famous cameo appearances in his
films that appear to have little relevance to the surrounding context.
However, the action has a very serious resonance. All three
characters will soon experience bullets in their heads, two literally
and one symbolically. Ben becomes deeply traumatized by the
actions he has to perform in the final part of the film that Woo
associates in his choice of editing with the violent consequences

Still 16   "Can friendship be measured in gold?"

following that earlier Saigon shooting witnessed also by Frank and Paul. In this context the "Mexican Stand-Off" gesture has a serious metaphorical meaning. It is not flamboyant showmanship. It emphasizes the accompanying dialogue stating the inherent humanitarian message of the film presented by a director fully conscious of its sad redundancy in a violent, material, and fallen world of the twentieth century and beyond. Exclusive devotion to monetary gain at the expense of friendship leads to death and destruction. Paul will not heed the message. He is well on his way to damnation as his lines reveal, "If I can't keep my gold, I might as well be dead." Like one of George Romero's atavistic zombies, Paul is now a living dead embodiment of social-Darwinist capitalist ideology.

Ben condemns his attitude. "How can you put gold before friendship? Don't friends mean anything to you anymore? Can friendship be measured in gold?" Frank begins throwing the gold away leading the pathetic Paul to break down. "This is all I've ever dreamed off: just these bars of gold. Nothing more." However, another invasion of violent forces occurs. The group faces further attack from their adversaries leading to the explosion of their boat in a manner paralleling the earlier destruction of the Saigon taxi containing smuggled penicillin. Ben attempts to persuade Paul to swim to safety. "The gold's too heavy. You will die. Forget about the gold." But this time, Paul will not allow his loot to disappear. While the other three swim to the shore and fight their enemies, Paul swims back to rescue his gold, an action emphasized in the original version of the film which also contains the comment of Frank who rescues him from drowning, "Damn your gold. If I'd known, I wouldn't have bothered saving you." However, this time they will not only have their ARVN opponents to deal with. The equally brutal forces of the North Vietnamese Army and the Viet Cong arrive. Separated from the others and recognizing that they will soon be outnumbered, Luke decides to run for cover and return to rescue his companions. The North Vietnamese surround Ben, Frank, and Paul. Predictably Paul complains that their search for Luke and calls to him have only resulted in their capture. "Shit! Why did we look for Luke?"

The next scene opens in a prison camp operated by the North Vietnamese Army and the Viet Cong. Like the "Russian Roulette" sequence in Cimino's *The Deer Hunter* (1977), the following images represent a nightmare scenario. But they are not gratuitous displays of violence. They rather represent the pivotal moment towards which the film has been moving symbolically evoking the "worst nightmare" scenario on the part of contemporary Hong Kong audiences as to what *might* happen after 1997. As one of the last colonies of a British Empire that humiliated China in the nineteenth century, the capitalist territory of Hong Kong had much to fear at the time of *Bullet in the Head*. Who knew whether the supposedly benevolent regime of Deng Xiaoping would remove its sheep's clothing to reveal its true form as a Maoist Cultural Revolution vengeful wolf eager to punish its orphan children for embracing Western values? Many Hong Kong people feared that they would be deemed collaborators, whether by association with the C.I.A., capitalism, the decadent values of Western culture, or by not handling contradictions in the correct Maoist manner. Every Hong Kong inhabitant became fair game for any future retribution — or so most people thought in 1990. Although this dreaded payback did not happen in 1997, this nevertheless should not lead us to deny the existence of such feelings following Tiananmen Square.

The prison camp sequence opens with Ben, Frank, and Paul imprisoned at night. In the background, a North Vietnam Officer discovers C.I.A. documents hidden in the bullion box Paul has perversely kept in his possession. Witnessing random executions of prisoners including ARVN soldiers, Americans, and Leong's Saigon associates, the young men again vainly attempt to assert their identity as Hong Kong Chinese. While Ben and Frank remain silent about their relationship to the gold bullion, Paul's greed again gets the better of him. "Yes, the gold is mine." This lands them in further trouble. They undergo another round of physical and psychological torture.

The next day, the NVA Officer begins his own version of a deadly game by forcing an American G.I. to shoot other captives. The man breaks down after his third killing before he himself dies under enemy fire. This event foreshadows Frank's descent into insanity. He will also emotionally break down after killing his third victim. The officer chooses Frank as his next victim. As in the Bolero Club scene when Frank affirmed his vain hope that "nobody gets killed," he again expresses his feelings to Ben. "I don't want to kill anybody." By contrast, Ben realizes the nature of the deadly game they confront. "We can't die here. We must go back to Hong Kong." He will direct his friend in a much more deadly version of a dance of death ironically paralleling his role in the film's credit sequence where he teaches students dance routines. The stakes are now much higher. The cross of salvation seen earlier in the church hall is now absent. Ben attempts to save his friend from physical harm. But any hope of spiritual redemption becomes impossible. They will both become damned in one way or another. By contrast, Paul has already joined the legion of the damned since he has sold his soul to the demonic realm of monetary gain. Ben prompts Frank, "They are just playing games" and (in one shot missing from the theatrical versions) tells him, "Shoot him or they will kill you." Frank fires his first shot. He tries to perform like a killing machine following the instructions of Ben, his director, before collapsing into hysteria. He fires his second bullet and again emotionally breaks down to the amusement of his captors. Ben attempts to encourage him. In another deleted shot, he tells Frank, "You must be strong." By contrast, the cynical Paul cries, "Don't give a shit. Keep shooting" before finally giving up on his friend and volunteering false information to the enemy to save himself. After the third killing, a crazed look appears on Frank's face anticipating that violent mask he will wear as a demented Saigon drug-addicted killer later in the film (Still 17). This once gentle person begins his eventual collapse into psychopathological violence that his supposed friend Paul will later finalize by firing a bullet into his head. Blood splatters on Frank's face following his third killing. Woo ironically subverts the idea of Christian baptism by revealing that Frank will become "born again" in a more deadly persona. The director depicts a satanic baptism by blood in a grim scene where no audience gratuitous indulgence in violent actions is really possible. It is a dark episode of apocalyptic violence beginning a devastating excessive psychological collapse for Frank far more traumatic than anything ever seen within the melodramatic imagination of either Eastern or Western generic incarnations. Frank becomes the first unwilling victim of a chaos world whose origins lie in the historical past of a Vietnam era that may also return to haunt Hong Kong in the imminent future.

Still 17   Frank begins his descent into the world of chaos.

Jacky Cheung's performance in this scene represents one of the film's great achievements. Woo extracts a great acting performance from a youngster then known for Cantopop ballads and teen romance comedies. It could easily have descended into grotesque dimensions. As an ugly representation of hideous violence having traumatic consequences for perpetrator as well as victim, this scene shows Woo's artistic and moral superiority far above anything that Quentin Tarantino and his imitators could ever aspire to — assuming that they showed any such interest in exploring the dark implications within the violence they celebrate.[24] In earlier VHS releases of this film, the "*Bullet in the Head*" main theme formed a grim accompanying note to these scenes showing Frank reluctantly forced into being a killer. This theme does not appear in later VHS and DVD versions of this film where Frank's actions occur without music. They remain ugly and violent. However, despite whatever reasons existed for removing the soundtrack, I would argue that its presence represents a crucial element inherent towards really appreciating the important structure of *Bullet in the Head*. It unites the apocalyptic and melodramatic aspects of the film in terms of emotional excess. Frank engages reluctantly in violent acts representing an apocalyptic nightmare vision of the worst aspects of a yet-to-happen 1997. The violence is neither gratuitous nor random. It represents Woo's version of humanity's dark descent into a violent world lacking any form of redemption or salvation whether Buddhist, Christian, or humanitarian. Frank descends into his own form of personal hell. His emotional collapse and his reversion into atavistic brutality represent his own particular melodramatic crisis.

Melodrama is a genre relevant to male as well as female crisis. This is particularly so in Eastern culture. Many past and present examples of Chinese cinema reveal this characteristic. Like several Stanley Kubrick characters, Frank descends into his own form of atavistic violence far removed from those bonds of friendship he displayed in Hong Kong and Saigon. His spiritual descent within the hell of the prison camp foreshadows his final drug-addicted damnation on the mean streets of Saigon. However, unlike Kubrick, Woo cannot view Frank's psychological collapse in a clinically dispassionate manner. He suffers along with his characters and makes his audiences, especially those who view the film seriously and sympathetically, feel similar emotions.[25]

Once Ben sees that Frank cannot take any more suffering and may become the next victim of any chosen assassin, he volunteers to take his place. "I hate the Americans. I'll kill them." Several DVD versions represent him swearing in Cantonese under his breath, one oath's translation anticipating the frequent profane word used both by Anthony Hopkins in *Nixon* (1999) and Ian McShane in the HBO TV series *Deadwood* (2005–2007). The former dance director now takes the stage like James Cagney in that accidental climactic moment in *Footlight Parade* (1933). But now his performance will be much deadlier than that of his Hollywood predecessor. Ben laughs with his tormentors as he uses a rifle to kill selected victims, both American and ARVN. Like Frank, he screams in agony as he kills his first victim, then laughs with his tormentors as if directing himself in his own form of murderous spectacular performance. Ben now becomes an actor-director but within a bloodthirsty scenario over which he has no control. He has to perform according to the demands of his Vietnamese captors who function like producers controlling their own version of a violent Category III film production. However, Ben also closes his eyes before firing the first shot. He is conscious of disturbing dehumanizing powers lying dormant within his own personality that could overwhelm him at any time during this deadly game. When ordered to kill Frank, Ben conceals his true feelings by laughing along with his oppressors, affirming, "Why not?" and requesting a pistol to replace the rifle he has emptied. He again curses his oppressors in Cantonese and also uses this language unknown to the North Vietnamese to reveal his true intentions to Frank by reaffirming his pledge to take him home. Ben then surprises his adversaries by killing those surrounding Frank and capturing the officer responsible for their torment by holding a gun to his head. Paul also seizes his moment by shooting his interrogators, placing the hand of another under the heavy weight of the bullion box before killing him, and escaping with his desired loot. He shows no intention of finding his friends.

However, unlike Paul, another friend arrives from the dead to rescue those he feels a close commitment towards. Dressed in jungle fatigues, Luke leads an American raiding party into the camp. He watches from a distance Ben's descent into atavistic violence. Angered at his tormentor, Ben fires a bullet into his head. He had earlier expressed his rage at another avatar from hell in the Bolero Club by pouring urine over his head. But, like Frank, Ben begins his own form of descent into a world of apocalyptic violence. Woo films this shot in slow motion evoking that earlier sequence showing the death of the Viet Cong suspect in the Catholic school playground. He also died from a bullet in the head. Although justified under the circumstances, Ben's actions now make him victimizer rather than victim. Ben continues firing bullets into his persecutor's dead body in frenzy until Luke appears in the scene to stop him as Frank would have done were he present. "Ben! Ben! Let go!" Meanwhile Frank searches for the most unworthy member of the group who resents his very presence. As the Viet Cong rally against the American invaders, Paul attempts to preserve his gold from anyone who gets in his way, even a close friend such as Frank who has just saved him from death in the same way he protected him during the Saigon robbery. Frank pleads with Paul to abandon the box and go in search of Ben. Instead, Paul wishes to silence his friend who now suffers from wounds incurred by protecting him from death by the North Vietnamese a few seconds before. Paul attempts to cover Frank's cries by covering his head with a jacket that only causes suffocation and further cries for help. Paul then decides to eliminate any remaining bonds he once had with Frank. "It's you or me. I don't have a choice." Using the accompanying sound of an explosion to muffle his shot, Paul fires a bullet through

Frank's head (Still 18). Luke witnesses this incident. Although injured by an explosion, he manages to get Frank to the safety of a helicopter.

Still 18   Paul's violent betrayal of Frank.

Escape and Brief Encounter

Ben goes in pursuit of Paul and his loot. Meanwhile Paul finds a boat and massacres the unarmed inhabitants of a North Vietnamese village who get in his way. By contrast, Ben gets in the way of Paul's bullets by using his body to conceal the naked body of a Vietnamese child.[26] After shooting anyone in sight, Paul starts the motor of the boat and begins his journey back to a prosperous future in Hong Kong. Following his departure, a group of Buddhist monks arrive and believe everyone is dead until they discover Ben. He begins a long process of recovery. Although the succeeding scenes were probably much longer in Woo's original version, the remaining brief images of the peaceful Buddhist countryside not only evoke memories of those idyllic landscapes seen in King Hu's *Come Drink with Me* (1965) and Zhang Che's very different sequel *Golden Swallow* (1968) but also those alternative realms of spiritual meditation common to other King Hu films such as *A Touch of Zen* (1969) and *Raining in the Mountain* (1979). Like the Cross symbol in the opening credits of *Bullet in the Head*, the Buddhist countryside sanctuary represents a spiritual contrast to an outside world contaminated by power and violence (Still 19). Several brief shots reveal the healing presence of nature. Water drips from a leaf into a bowl containing petals. These scenes appear as evocative as those nature sequences in *A Touch of Zen* with the notable exception that no threatening spider and web imagery appear.[27] Woo, instead, appears to emphasize the lyrical landscape of King Hu's masterpiece seen in its introductory images revealing an alternative utopian peaceful realm available to humanity but very rarely found in everyday life. Ben recovers. One scene shows him sitting in silent contemplation. Above him, a flock of white birds fly, evoking Woo's frequent references to the dove as a symbol of peace. These peaceful moments represent the director's version of Eisenstein's tranquil "Appeal from the Dead" sequence in *Battleship Potemkin* (1925) that provides a break between the violent action of the first half of the film and the even more brutal images of the Potemkin Steps massacre sequence. One expects Roy Chaio's Buddhist abbot Hui

Still 19 Ben experiences a peaceful world.

Yan from *A Touch of Zen* to appear at any moment during this time when Ben finds true peace. But he cannot remain. He has promised Frank that they will return to Hong Kong. But the Frank he finds is not the one he has previously known.

When Ben returns to Luke's house, he finds his Eurasian friend another victim of the Vietnam War, missing his right arm. Despite his dismemberment barring him from any further excursions into his previous career, Luke appears at peace with himself. "Everyone has to sacrifice in this war." He tells Ben about Frank's current condition: "He's not the same Frank. I wish I hadn't brought him back." Woo briefly cuts to a side view of the traumatized Frank sitting agitated in a Saigon street at night wearing military fatigues marking him as another victim/victimizer of the conflict. He also represents another of John Woo's human casualties trapped within his form of personal damnation. Woo later visually emphasizes Frank's tormented condition in an overhead moving camera shot looking down at him from a hole in the ceiling as if comparing him to one of Dante's doomed souls from *The Divine Comedy* trapped within the inner circle of Hell. Paul's bullet still remains in his head. Frank is now a murderous embodiment of the walking wounded of the Vietnam War. The bullet causes him intense mental and physical agony which he can only alleviate temporarily by morphine injections purchased from the money he now earns from his new occupation as a hired killer. Frank demonically embodies Luke's former persona. He wears the same type of military fatigues worn by Luke during his attack on the Viet Cong camp and identifies his victims using the same method Luke once did by looking at a photo before shooting them. While Luke obtains spiritual peace by being removed from the contamination of his former profession, Frank ironically takes his vacant place as a monstrous alter-ego.

Woo depicts Frank's new character in imagery reminiscent of a horror film. Like a Frankenstein monster, Frank is a silent, speechless automaton walking towards his victim against an expressionistically lit urban background. His slow movement evokes those menacing steps associated with Boris Karloff in James Whale's *Frankenstein* (1931). He is now a killing machine having lost all his former qualities of humanity. Frank's condition results from Paul's economic greed. He also traumatically suffers from the effects of the Vietnam War. Frank is now a lost soul. After Frank has killed his assigned victim by repeatedly firing shots into his dead body in the same manner Ben did to the North Vietnam officer in the prison camp, he collapses by the side of his victim's car right of frame. Woo then makes a barely noticeable transition to another shot showing Frank crawling to a different car left of frame that makes it seem that the actions form part of the same shot. Money and violence represent symbiotic forms of blood brotherhood. An unseen figure throws money at Frank paying him for his service before driving off. Contrary to his previous actions when he ignored the money from Paul's robbery or generously passed currency to fleeing Vietnamese refugees, Frank picks up the scattered notes and crawls towards a drug pusher. Supplied with morphine from the entire amount of money he earned from his assassination, Frank staggers into an alley and injects his arm for temporary relief from pain. Woo concludes this sequence by a lap dissolve from Frank in the alley to a soft focus shot of Luke in the background and a sharp focus one of Ben in the foreground. He uses similar shots in the film to stress close bonding between various protagonists in the film. While Frank earlier felt responsible for disrupting his friend's wedding night in Hong Kong by an act of violence, Ben now feels responsible for the plight of a former friend he brought to Vietnam in the first place.

Luke takes Ben to his friend's lair and informs him that Frank will eventually become a vegetable since it is now impossible to remove the bullet from his head. Ben discovers that Frank is now a speechless, violent monster who fires bullets recklessly at anyone he feels will take his drugs away from him. Helped by Luke, Ben appeals to what remains of his close friend. He tries to get some reaction from him by evoking past memories. Ben attempts to get Frank to remember his earlier generous practices of sharing things by looking at the morphine needle. "You didn't give me any. Don't you remember there were good times and bad times. You never shared your bad times with me. We agreed to share everything in life. We were like brothers since we were kids. You called me brother all the time. But friends are always equal ... You got so many scars on your head. You were beaten by your mother because you were so naughty so she wanted to beat you up ... If it had not been for you we could not have afforded to get married." Although a faint glimmer of recognition appears on Frank's face, he cannot speak to Ben in the way he once could have done. "I'd just like to listen to you, just a few words." Ben finally recognizes that his friend is really a lost soul who can never regain his former personality. During this time, Luke remains silently in the background. He hands Ben his gun to put Frank out of his misery (Still 20). Ben makes a last appeal to Frank. "I don't want to do it. But I can't bear to see you like this." This is another poignant sequence in the film. The main "*Bullet in the Head*" theme now plays softly in the background. It both evokes a lost world of past memories as well

Still 20   Frank's farewell to Ben.

as underscores by its sad refrain the tragic necessity of an act Ben will have to perform. These intuitively sensitive and touching features that occur in this part of *Bullet in the Head* owe much to Woo's direction and the accomplished performances of Jackie Cheung and Tony Leung.

Woo films Frank's last moments in an exemplary manner. It reveals him as a great director of silent cinema as well as a major twentieth-century talent. Like Howard Hawks in the opening sequence of *Rio Bravo* (1959) and Alfred Hitchcock's pure cinematic silent moments in *Notorious* (1946) and *Marnie* (1964), Woo dispenses entirely with dialogue. He shoots a scene utilizing key elements from a lost cinematic art form and also calls on the audience to participate emotionally in the scene.[28] Only one remedy can end the suffering of a tormented soul. In a close-up shot, Ben initially holds the gun to Frank's head but Frank makes a gesture indicating that he does not want another bullet in his head. Instead, he moves the gun to his heart. Using a second close-up, Woo films the bullet penetrating Frank's chest in slow motion. This occurs less as a spectacular indulgence in violent special effects but more in the manner of underscoring the poignancy of a deed that is tragically necessary. It is emotionally devastating. The final farewell between Ben and Frank also occurs in close-up. In his final seconds of life, Frank looks up at his friend. His face reveals a slight glimmer of recognition. He faintly smiles for the last time. Woo then freeze frames the image as he did on that wedding banquet night many years ago when three young men were united in friendship. But this time, one is absent. A gun ominously appears from below the right frame before the image freezes. Its appearance can have several meanings. They range from ironically symbolizing the presence of a "missing friend" who used violence against Frank to embody Ben's altruistically different use of a weapon that now brings peace to a tormented soul. It is also metaphor for the film's final reckoning.

Ben bids farewell to Luke who has decided to remain in Saigon. The two friends part for the last time. Luke now appears at peace with himself. He is physically scarred with his face displaying burns from an explosion during the time he rescued Frank. But he is also internally purified having undergone spiritual redemption by rescuing Frank. He chooses not to take up Ben's offer to return to Hong Kong. He will remain to see what his better tomorrow will bring.

The final scene of this act involves several epic shots showing Ben as a refugee in the midst of Vietnamese civilians with an American military escort fleeing enemy bombing during daytime. Again, the omnipresent tank of the earlier night attack sequence appears along with a reprise of the film's main musical theme that had accompanied the previous appearance of this incarnation of American military power. But its force is now diminished by North Vietnamese guerilla activity. Although many distributors regarded this scene as redundant and eagerly removed it for slowing down the narrative and delaying Ben's final encounter with Paul, it is an integral part of the film. It reveals Ben as a victim of overwhelming historical forces affecting individual destiny. The sequence prematurely evokes the Fall of Saigon anticipated in earlier shots during demonstration scenes showing Vietnamese trying to climb the gates of the American embassy to seek refuge inside. In 1990, audiences already knew what happened to those South Vietnamese who missed the last helicopter that departed from the embassy roof. Would they also become refugees after 1997 in the same way that their grandparents and parents were after 1949 and during succeeding decades, particularly those following the dark years of the Cultural Revolution?

The Final Reckoning

The last act begins. A lap dissolve from the preceding refugee sequence returns Ben to Hong Kong three years later. Credits display the date "1970." Ben stands before Jane's family stall, the very place where three young men had spoken about leaving Hong Kong in a now distant past. Ben not only reunites with Jane but also discovers a son he has never seen, intuitively named by its mother after one who had acted as a best friend by bringing them together. After his traumatic experiences, Ben could settle down with his family. However, he has one final duty to perform.

One earlier version of the film concluded with a different depiction of the boardroom confrontation between Ben and Paul. There Ben shoots Paul in the head in revenge for his treatment of Frank before a group of Triad businessmen. After this final shot, the screen goes black and the credits roll. Although John Charles and Bey Logan regard this version as having "a much more emotionally satisfying climax" in a film needing "to end on a whimper and not a bang," I wish to argue in favor of the conclusion that is now in circulation both theatrically and on DVD.[29] The other ending appears more arbitrary in nature and abruptly terminates a film needing the type of developed resolution that will occur in the car battle between Ben and Paul ironically evoking that earlier bike ride sequence that occurred in Hong Kong many years before. *Bullet in the Head* is a film carefully structured on dualities and parallels. The current ending is essential towards understanding its meaning.

The boardroom sequence begins by showing Paul (with Waise Lee without a hairpiece making him look much younger in the rest of the film) about to realize his ambition of being number one.[30] Waiting for the call to take over, he looks at a globe and spins it around as if anticipating Triad globalization dreams of world domination.[31] His action also echoes his earlier lines in the film,

"There's no going back. The whole world will be ours." Paul believes that he has eliminated his former partners. But they will return to haunt him, one living, another dead. At the boardroom meeting, Mr. Kwan announces his retirement in favor of Paul (perhaps conscious of Waise Lee's removal of another elderly boss in *A Better Tomorrow*!). He speaks of Paul's business success in laundering money and preventing government prosecution. Ben arrives and is granted admittance. Initially shocked at seeing him alive, Paul embraces his former friend and makes his last economic offer. "Half my money is yours." Ben, instead, causes Paul to "lose face" amongst the Triads by revealing to them his guilty secret: Frank's skull (Still 21). He has promised to bring his friend home. "Why did you not shoot straight? Now he has to suffer more. Is a friend only worth a box of gold to you?" Ben's words state that Frank's spirit is still in turmoil. He condemns his friend for betraying traditional Chinese values involving not only friendship but causing the suffering of someone in the afterlife who cannot rest until a final reckoning is made against one who committed the unholy deed of betrayal. Paul refuses to accept responsibility. "There are dead people lying around everywhere. You can bring back any bone and say it is Frank."

Still 21   Ben confronts Paul with evidence of his betrayal.

In the alternative ending, Ben confronts Paul with his guilty deed, wraps his head in his jacket (in the same way Paul did to Frank in Vietnam) and fires a bullet into his head. But this particular ending would leave too many loose endings. Would Ben be able to escape the vengeance of Paul's Triad associates? As documented research on the Triads shows, the organization's emphasis on loyalty is more a matter of word rather than deed as Johnnie To's *Election* films reveal. Even if the Triads did not execute Ben for killing one of their own he has committed a murder in front of witnesses and could be delivered to the police. At least the present ending in circulation allows Ben the chance of finally returning to his family. Also, although the succeeding car battle between Ben and Paul may resemble a redundant display of Woo pyrotechnics, it appropriately complements the rest of the film. *Bullet in the Head* needs to move towards an apocalyptic type of violent resolution in keeping with the rest of its narrative.

Ben lies in wait in a car with Frank's skull beside him. Paul enters an indoor car park with his Triad associates and enters the Mercedes he has always dreamed of owning since his days as a poor youngster in Hong Kong. Like Ti Lung in *Blood Brothers*, he has to pay the price for his betrayal. Woo cuts between shots of the earlier harmless bike ride race between the friends and the more deadly Uzi/handgun battle between Ben and Paul as their cars race towards Ching Yu docks (Still 22). However, Woo does not merely intend to contrast these scenes but also intimate that from the beginning Paul's competitive spirit has formed a barrier to true friendship. Then, as now, he wishes to win and tolerates no obstacle in his path. His dialogue in the flashback sequence and his present taunts to Ben reveal this. After Ben crashes into Paul's Mercedes, the latter taunts him. "You want to take revenge but I am never a loser in my life. They did not kill me in Vietnam. See if you can now. We are fugitives in all our lives. See who runs out of luck now. I always win." The chase occurs against an inferno-esque background of constant explosions that conclude when Paul's Mercedes finally erupts into flames. Ben discovers that Frank's skull is missing from the car seat. As he searches for it, Paul shoots him. Paul then sees Frank's skull and speaks to it. His blood-splattered frenzied face reveals a man totally possessed not by evil spirits but corrupt twentieth-century forces of money, power, and violence (Still 23). The blood on his face also evokes that earlier scene of blood splashing on his face when he killed his third victim in Mr. Leong's Bolero Club. This ironically made Frank and Paul blood

Still 22   The car battle between Ben and Paul.

Still 23   The damned soul of Paul.

brothers in an apocalyptic world of violence since Frank's face also became sprayed by blood when he shot a prisoner in the Viet Cong camp. Several critics condemn the hysterical performance of Waise Lee at this point of the film but this is misguided. Lee's performance here embodies another example of Woo's melodramatic masculine crisis that appears throughout *Bullet in the Head* as well as in *A Better Tomorrow 1* and *2* and *The Killer*. The director not only takes his audience into the realms of Jacobean revenge tragedy but also within those dark areas of the human soul depicted in Peckinpah's *Bring Me the Head of Alfredo Garcia* (1974). Like Warren Oates's venal Benny, Paul has caused the death of someone once close to him and becomes forever haunted by the head of Alfredo Garcia. Paul now becomes afraid of Frank's skull and speaks to it in a manner evoking Oates's earlier possessed performance in Peckinpah's twentieth-century version of the American Gothic (Still 24).

Still 24   A moment of Shakespearean tragedy.

"You died. Why don't you leave me alone? You brought it on yourself. You are a dead man to want to follow me. Your spirit is angry. I'll give you rest." But, instead of shooting another bullet into Frank's skull, Paul makes Ben pull the trigger. "He says he's not satisfied. Let us help him die." Paul's lines to Ben reveal his guilty recognition of what he has done despite his self-interested plea to Ben to perform one last act of friendship before they finally separate. "Ben, we must die together. Come on, my friend. Give him one more shot so he can rest in peace. Then he won't suffer anymore." During these lines, Woo inserts earlier sequences of Paul shooting Frank in the head in Vietnam, an act also representing selfish motivations. His other lines to Ben emphasize that self-interest rather than guilt motivates him. "I'll go on making more money and you can make another friend." After Ben fires the bullet, Frank's skull moves into one of the fires that have started as a result of the nearby exploding oil cans. These fires give the environment hellish connotations. By forcing Ben to fire a bullet into Frank's skull Paul makes him perform an act Frank did not want him to do in his last seconds of life. Paul now pollutes Ben's soul by making him perform this action. He is again manipulating a friend for his own selfish reasons but this will be for the last time. Ben reacts by grabbing Paul and shooting him through the head, an act that Woo contrasts by inserting earlier scenes of Ben shooting the North Vietnamese officer through the head and enjoying his bloody revenge until Luke arrived to save him. This time Luke is not present to save him. Instead, Paul falls to the ground in peaceful repose as if grateful for his own release from a living hell that polluted his soul.[32]

Epilogue

Ben now has to live with the consequences of his final act of violence. He screams in agony. It recalls that moment in the Viet Cong prison camp when he screamed briefly after being forced to kill his first vulnerable victim. Ben throws away his gun and walks into the distance. Dawn slowly breaks on the horizon faintly penetrating flames of apocalyptic violence. Paul's body lies in the foreground while Frank's skull lies within a fiery funeral pyre (Still 25). The melancholy sounds of the film's main theme occur for the last time. Ben may walk away a free man. But he will be forever contaminated by the violent events that have affected him throughout the entire film. *Bullet in the Head* represents Woo's recognition that his final "last hurrah for chivalry" is now entirely redundant in the dark world of a closing twentieth century.

Still 25   The final chapter.

Theatrical Structure of *Bullet in the Head*

(Prologue: Credit sequences, friendship, romance, and violence.)

Act One:

Scene one:	The wedding
Scene two:	Frank's pledge and the reaffirmation of blood brotherhood
Scene three:	The revenge on Ringo and the planned departure to Vietnam
Scene four:	Ben's farewell to Jane

Act Two:

Scene one: Arrival in Saigon and the "Tet Offensive Bullet in the Head"
Scene two: In the lair of Mr. Leung
Scene three: Paul's robbery
Scene four: The second demonstration: echoes of loss and Tiananmen Square
Scene five: The Bolero Club massacre
Scene six: Escape by night

Act Three:

Scene one: The death of Sally
Scene two: Confrontation and capture by the North Vietnamese
Scene three: Apocalyptic moments of violence
Scene four: The last meeting of Ben and Frank
Scene five: Farewell to Luke
Scene six: The long journey home

Act Four:

Scene one: The return to Jane
Scene two: The reckoning
Scene three: The battle with Paul

3

Aftermath

John Woo shot *Bullet in the Head*'s first part in those rapidly disappearing Hong Kong locations that evoked the film's period setting in the 1960s. He particularly featured in the early scenes contemporary seven-storey lower-class estates that would be replaced by high-rise apartment blocks over two decades later. By contrast with his deliberate choice of period locations, the first part of the battle between Ben and Paul occurs in an indoor car park that has been used as a location for countless Hong Kong action films before and since. This is highly appropriate in emphasizing the dehumanizing aspects of a twentieth-century material world that Paul has entered. If Shakespeare's damned monarch utters the immortal lines, "A horse! A horse! My kingdom for a horse" in his closing lines in Act V, scene iv of *Richard III*, Paul uses his own Mercedes that he once dreamed about owning in his early days in Hong Kong to fight Ben who drives another car. Woo also used Thailand for the Vietnam sequences with the exception of the Bolero Club interior scenes which were filmed in Golden Harvest

Studios. Following his break with Tsui Hark, he decided to go ahead and shoot his own version of a Vietnam film originally scheduled as a Film Workshop production to follow his successful *A Better Tomorrow* films. Despite lacking the financial resources of Film Workshop, Woo decided to proceed and act as his own producer having to raise the money himself. According to one source, he "financed almost all of the cost of the movie out of his own pocket" making its budget one of the highest at the time for any contemporary Hong Kong film resulting in a cost of approximately US $3.5 million.[1] It became a deeply personal project and the one film Woo would like to be remembered for today. The original cut ran nearly three hours but the Golden Princess Film Distribution Company became concerned at its excessive length and demanded that Woo edit the film down to a commercially acceptable level that would involve as many screenings a day possible. Woo's final cut ran roughly for some 136 minutes. The film circulated in different lengths according to the demands of local censorship requirements and distributors wanting the shortest version possible to emphasize Woo's action sequences rather than a longer version with deeper meanings. Theatrical, laser, VHS, and VCD versions could run for as little as 100 minutes or as long as 130. A comparison of the original movie trailer with its second edited version is also instructive. The first emphasizes historical and political elements while the second limits this footage to promote instead a recognizable generic product that producers believed Hong Kong audiences would readily accept.[2]

Bullet in the Head premiered on September 9, 1990. Released during a period when apprehension over Tiananmen Square and its relationship to the imminent 1997 return to the Mainland evoked concern on the part of Hong Kong's population, it failed at the box office and may not have covered its costs at the time. Looking forward to Chinese New Year local audiences were seeking light relief. A film reminding them of an ugly historical incident a year before would not provide this. As Stephen Teo notes, *Bullet in the Head* may be "Woo's most extreme representation of male bonding but it also revealed Hong Kong people's capacity for courage, cowardice, and greed. Behind all this lurks 1997."[3] Woo also stressed that the film reflected his emotional feelings about the Tiananmen Square massacre and defended the somber and serious nature of a work that was far bleaker than his previous post-1987 films. "In this film I wanted to address something that was happening in Hong Kong or will happen in Hong Kong. Wartime Vietnam was a metaphor for all this."[4] Interviewing Woo, Teo noted that "Woo pointed out that the film had a tragic tone and was utterly devoid of heroes, while audiences could sense that wartime Vietnam functioned as a metaphor for their own predicament, having filled their spiritual void with materialistic greed."[5] Although Terence Chang was not directly involved with the film, he understood what his friend intended. In a later interview he ironically mentions that "John Woo attempted to put his personal feelings towards 1997 in *Bullet in the Head*, but unfortunately most Hong Kong people identified with the Waise Lee character and thought he was the real hero of the movie."[6] Unlike Paul, Woo has frequently revealed his own qualities of integrity by still defending his most personal project to date despite the fact that it disappointed the commercial requirements of Hollywood and Hong Kong by not making money at the box office.

> I don't think anyone in Hong Kong was in the mood to see the picture more than once, which is necessary in a small market like Hong Kong to make money on a picture, and so they stayed away. But I still consider this my favorite movie because of how much I poured into it.[7]

Bullet in the Head suffered from the same type of reception as the Vietnam syndrome in America during the period of the actual war. With the exception of *The Green Berets* (1968), no Hollywood film explicitly dealing with the conflict appeared during 1964–1975 but this did not prevent the appearance of veiled representations appearing in a diverse number of genres.[8] Hong Kong cinema also engaged in its own type of allegorical representations of 1997. The issue had been in the mind of its inhabitants ever since British Prime Minister Thatcher signed over the colony to eventual control by the Mainland in the 1980s agreement.[9] *Bullet in the Head* failed at the box office because it presented the dark overtones of what might happen in a far more explicitly violent sense than any film at the time or later. By contrast Tsui Hark's *A Better Tomorrow 3* (1989) prequel is far too indebted to the action movie dynamics of Hong Kong cinema and does not have the type of ugly overtones that occur in scenes of Frank's being forced to shoot helpless captives. Hark's film also dwells too much on the melodramatic aspects of the romantic triangular relationship between the three major characters while Woo's version involving Ben, Luke, and Sally is far more integrated into the narrative of a film dealing with the serious implications of male friendship. In *A Better Tomorrow 3*, the action sequences, well directed as they are, tend to be more isolated within the context of the film as spectacular set pieces that Hong Kong audiences would expect. By contrast, Woo's depictions of action reveal dark elements that tend to undercut the type of audience gratification accompanying such scenes. Woo also reworked the "Russian Roulette" sequence from *The Deer Hunter* for his own creative purposes in a far more accomplished manner than Cimino's earlier recreation. Simon Yam remarked that the Vietnam experience was foreign to Hong Kong audiences and this explained the disappointing box-office reaction. While Pearl Harbor has a particular resonance for American audiences, Hong Kong does not have such experience. The colony has never fought in any war nor experienced its effects so audiences did not have that type of relationship to the events on screen. Co-scenarist Patrick Leung also recognized that local audiences were looking forward to the Chinese New Year and expecting a "happy movie" as a form of escape.[10]

As Jacky Cheung and Bey Logan point out, the film had no major stars. Tony Leung, Jacky Cheung, and Simon Yam were not the well-known names they are now at the time of *Bullet in the Head*'s release.[11] Despite this, Leung and Woo felt that the use of non-stars would bring more reality into a film intended to be stylistically different from the director's recent films. Unlike *A Better Tomorrow*, *Bullet in the Head* was designed to be more realistic than romantic. Both Leung and Woo knew of Jackie Cheung's performance in Wong Kar-wai's *As Tears Go By* (1988) that revealed he was more than a Cantopop idol. Woo also based the character very much on his own younger brother. Waise Lee became the "calculating traitor who betrays his friends" while Simon Yam's more romantic performance was designed to be the sugar covering Woo's more realistic approach throughout the entire film.[12] However, the initial response to the film was hostile. Faced with demands to reduce the film's length for Hong Kong audiences, Woo used the boardroom confrontation scene between Ben and Paul that he had shot first and concluded it with Ben shooting Paul in the head before the Triads in the boardroom. According to Terence Chang, the film originally ended here with a fade to black.[13] But other distributors wished for a more recognizable John Woo conclusion.

Additional action footage choreographed by Philip Kwok resulted in the showing of a final gun battle between Ben and Paul. Stills exist showing Woo rehearsing Tony Leung and Waise Lee for the final bullet in the head scene. Strict censorship in Malaysia also resulted in the elimination of other scenes, among which was perhaps the infamous urine drinking sequence. Patrick Leung also mentions that certain political references were not allowed by Taiwanese censorship so they also ended up on the cutting room floor. However, the Long Shong Productions Taiwan release version was more comprehensive than the Hong Kong versions. It also contained the main musical theme by James Wong and Romeo Diaz accompanying Frank's shooting of the hostages in the Viet Cong camp, giving the depiction a much more apocalyptic melodramatic resonance than any of the versions currently available. Like Woo's use of "I'm a Believer," the film's main theme was never designed as mere background music. It reoccurs with significant variations throughout the film underscoring the emotional resonance of each particular scene that it accompanies. A lyrical version emphasizes the carefree youthful lives of three close friends in the early Hong Kong scenes. The mood becomes more somber later and highly emotional as seen in the two Vietnam refugee scenes shot in night and day as well as the traumatic sequence showing Frank being forced by the North Vietnamese to murder helpless hostages and tragically being encouraged by Ben to do so. Frank is on his way to becoming the olive green Frankenstein monster Ben later discovers in Saigon who wishes his close friend to put him out of his misery almost as if he silently articulates those poignant final lines of Karloff in *The Bride of Frankenstein* (1935). "We belong dead." When Ben agrees to Frank's last request, the "*Bullet in the Head*" theme plays wistfully in the background as it had in those previous moments in which Ben vainly attempted to make his friend remember the past and respond to him. Frank does but not in the way Ben hoped for. Frank wishes Ben to perform one final act of friendship by putting him out of his misery so he can finally escape his tormented entrapment in a Saigon underworld that makes his life a living hell. *Bullet in the Head* is a carefully constructed film. Any missing scene involving visual representation or musical accompaniment represents a tragic loss in terms of understanding the full extent of John Woo's creative vision.

Unfortunately, no copy was ever made of the original version. Only fragments survive and we can only guess at how much is now lost. After fifteen years, memories of the missing material are now vague but Leong does recall that Woo shot many scenes showing Ben as a dance instructor. These scenes were also autobiographical since Woo had worked in a similar capacity to earn money when he was young.[14] However, since Woo has often spoken of the deliberate parallels that his carefully constructed action sequences have with the Hollywood musical, these missing scenes may have involved some key levels of meaning. *West Side Story* obviously influenced the fighting sequences seen during the credit sequences. Woo may have developed his own creative synthesis of employing those oppositional generic realms of ballet and violence that Robert Wise's film suggested.

Also, unlike *A Better Tomorrow 1* and *2* and *The Killer*, *Bullet in the Head* contained no unblemished heroic figures for audiences to identify with. Very few members of the audience who went to see the film because of Jacky Cheung's presence would accept a performance at odds with his celebrated Hong Kong romantic balladeer. As Bey Logan mentions in his DVD audio-commentary, it was equivalent to watching Clint Eastwood symbolically castrated in Don Siegel's *The Beguiled* (1970), another film that commercially flopped at the box office. The star returned in the more audience-friendly *Dirty Harry* (1971). Woo would make Hong Kong audiences "happy together" again with his 1991 lightweight action-romance *Once a Thief*.[15]

Bullet in the Head is an exceedingly grim film standing head and shoulders above anything Woo directed before and after. This comment is not designed to denigrate the director's earlier and later achievements but merely to emphasize that it cannot be easily compared to *A Better Tomorrow 1* and *2* and *The Killer*, to say nothing of Woo's later Hollywood films. Woo's recognition as auteur generally owed much to those stylistic action sequences that brought him to the attention of Hollywood and the dubious acclaim of figures such as Quentin Tarantino rather than the serious themes structuring his films. In 1992, Woo directed his last Hong Kong film, *Hard Boiled.* It reunited him with Chow Yun-fat and the actor he first used in *Bullet in the Head* — Tony Leung Chiu-wai. *Hard Boiled* combined Chow Yun-fat's particular brand of star charisma with the more complex acting talents of Tony Leung and Anthony Wong Chau-sang. Leung played an early version of the role he would later perform in *Infernal Affairs* (2002).[16] Although *Hard Boiled* contained serious themes, it was made as a crowd-pleaser to show that Woo could make a Hong Kong version of *Die Hard* (1988) and its ilk much better than any Hollywood director. Woo succeeded. He soon left for America, becoming one of many talents to flee from what he feared might happen in 1997.

Although Woo fulfilled the dream of many Hong Kong talents such as Jackie Chan to finally work in Hollywood, his position has not allowed him the type of creative freedom he once had in Hong Kong. Like many classical and post-classical Hollywood directors, he has found himself torn between the demands of the box office and his desire to make more personal films. Woo now finds himself trapped within the more constraining demands of a film industry dominated by hugely inflated big budget productions that do not allow him the same type of frequent work and experimentation with generic formulas that benefited directors in the old classical Hollywood studio system as well as his post-1986 films. Projects have arisen and collapsed for many reasons. Woo's Hollywood reunification with Chow Yun-fat in *King's Ransom* and his frequent attempts to revive King Hu's dream project about a film dealing with Chinese laborers who worked on American railroads in the nineteenth century have all remained distant dreams so far. Yet it is too early to dismiss Woo as having failed to live up to his Hong Kong promise in contemporary Hollywood. He is really at the middle stage of his career and has the possibility of making many other films. His Hollywood films may also need the type of re-evaluation that benefited critical appreciation of the American work of Alfred Hitchcock and Fritz Lang. They were once only recognized for their British and German films. The same process may occur with John Woo. He has directed crowd-pleasers such as *Broken Arrow* (1996), *MIA 2* (2001), and *Paycheck* (2003), as well as more intricate films such as *Hard Target* (1993), *Face/Off* (1999), and the unjustly neglected *Windtalkers* (2002). This last film urgently needs re-evaluation after its mistimed appearance following the jingoistic climate of 9/11 as well as its unjust shadowing by far inferior, successful box-office products such as *Pearl Harbor* (2004).[17] Woo may not have managed to continue his creative exploration into those dangerous historical and political forces affecting the human condition in his Hollywood productions as he did in *Bullet in the Head*. But films such as *Hard Target* and *Windtalkers* contain several relevant parallels to such earlier concerns existing beneath their respective generic frameworks. Despite the fact that *Paycheck* initially appears to be a run-for-cover project designed to counter the unfair critical and commercial reception of *Windtalkers*, it also involves the theme of a man refusing to sell his soul for money and deciding to oppose a dehumanizing capitalist corporate society that Paul in *Bullet* would have immediately embraced as his own monetarist Garden of Eden.

Woo is just another action film director in the eyes of the corporate Hollywood establishment. He is not recognized for being the serious artist that he is and this affects the funding of projects that would really reflect the complex nature of his talent. He is just another transnational artist brought into an industry that now shows little respect and understanding for creativity. Woo is celebrated less as the director of *Bullet in the Head* but more as an innovator of action sequences a jaded Hollywood seeks to appropriate after viewing those various stylistic and technical displays within *A Better Tomorrow 1* and *2*, *The Killer*, and *Hard Boiled*, but ignoring the more serious undertones existing within. However, *Bullet in the Head* continues to gain more critical appreciation over the course of time. It may eventually surpass *The Killer* in becoming recognized as the director's major creative achievement to date.

Woo still remains a Hong Kong director, a designation that is transnational as well as national. He belongs to a cinema that often borrows from outside only to transform external elements in a more creative manner that often surpass their initial appearances. In several interviews, he has spoken of his love for Hollywood cinema. He went to America to learn first hand about a different cinematic culture. During a recent interview, he has spoken of eventually returning to Hong Kong to make more films there as a result of his new experiences working in another culture. At the time of writing, he is in Mainland China filming one of his country's great national epics. As a Hong Kong–Hollywood director, he will probably bring a unique sensibility to this project creatively, fusing different cultural influences and having access to the far more accomplished and nuanced acting talents of Tony Leung Chiu-wai and Takeshi Kaneshiro whose Eastern performances far outmatch anything that an artistically stagnant Hollywood cinema can furnish today. *Red Cliff* will be his second epic. *Bullet in the Head* was an attempt at this type of production. Woo made *Bullet* as his particular version of a David Lean film influenced by his own cultural traditions as well as a particular historical moment of apocalyptic crisis whose moral lessons have yet to be understood. Whatever he will direct in the future, *Bullet in the Head* remains a film he has every reason to be proud of. It is a major achievement of Hong Kong cinema.

Appendix

The Different Versions of *Bullet in the Head*

John Woo's *Bullet in the Head* appeared in many different versions following the time of its original theatrical release in Hong Kong during August 17–31, 1990. No one cut is really definitive, not even the 136-minute versions now available on the Fortune Star/Joy Star DVD version (which contain fragments from missing footage that can be integrated into the running time or played separately) or the U.K. *Hong Kong Legends* DVD reissue of 2004. Although the case of *Bullet in the Head* does not resemble the nature of Orson Welles's original version of *The Magnificent Ambersons* (1942) or *Mr. Arkadin* (1955) which can be separated into seven different versions, the truth remains that no "director's cut" is now in existence nor, sadly, will there ever be one. This is also true of Fritz Lang's original versions of *Metropolis* (1927) and *Spione* (1928). The full version of *Bullet in the Head* is probably the nearest equivalent that Hong Kong cinema has to the missing version of *The Magnificent*

Ambersons both in terms of length and significant content, the only difference being that no complete screenplay is currently available by which we can attempt to recover the construction of the entire film. Hopefully, this may change in the future.

The first version (or "Ur" version) was John Woo's original cut that ran over three hours long. Golden Princess Film Production Company demanded that Woo reduce the film to a commercially viable running time. This probably emphasized the historical and political elements already implicit in the second version that may have been regarded as redundant for commercial purposes or capable of offending local censorship bodies.

The second version is the one theatrically distributed by Golden Princess Film Production Company that ran 136 minutes. Producers insisted that Woo also shoot some new sequences such as Ben's murder of Paul in the Triad boardroom and the final battle between both in the last ten minutes of the film. When the film received its first theatrical run, the last third resembled the versions available on DVD today where Ben leaves after making Paul lose "face" before the Triads and then waits to take revenge on him. However, local producers and distributors eager to gain as many screenings during the day would have insisted on further cuts leading to the next version.

The third version is the one that concludes most VCD copies. It is now available as an extra on the two DVD versions currently in circulation. After confronting Paul with Frank's skull in the boardroom, Ben suddenly pulls Paul's jacket over his head. Woo intercuts this with a shot of Paul's similar action to Frank in Vietnam. Traumatized by this memory, Ben gazes at Frank's skull on the table, and remembers Paul shooting Frank through the head as he hears the latter's screams. Woo then shoots a close-up of Ben's gun pointing at the back of Paul's head. He fires. The screen then fades to black and the credits roll. This version runs approximately 100 minutes.

A fourth version ran theatrically and later became distributed on some VHS copies that ran for 120 minutes. It cut out certain scenes regarded as inessential such as Ben's departure from South Vietnam with refugees accompanied by the American military.

As John Charles points out in his review of the film in his excellent encyclopedia, the running times could be as short as 100 minutes or as long as 130 depending on the venue, format, and country.

Wikipedia has an entry on *Bullet in the Head*: http://en. wikipedia.org/wiki/Bullet_in_the_Head.

It contains a list of some thirty-five scenes that characterize the different versions but many sequences are now lost for ever.

Notes

Acknowledgements

1   Ken Loach, "Director's Note." *The Wind That Shakes the Barley*. Cork, Ireland: Galley Head Press, 2006, 9.

Chapter 1   The Apocalyptic Moment of *Bullet in the Head*

1   See *Chang Che: A Memoir*. Ed. Wong Ain-ling. Hong Kong: Hong Kong Film Archive, 2004.
2   John Charles, *Hong Kong Filmography 1977–1997*. Jefferson, NC: McFarland & Co, 2000, 178; Stephen Teo, *Hong Kong Cinema: The Extra Dimensions*. London: BFI Publishing, 1997, 175; Lisa Odham Stokes and Michael Hoover, *City on Fire: Hong Kong Cinema*. London: Verso, 1999, 43–44; Kenneth E. Hall, *John Woo: The Films*. Jefferson, NC: McFarland & Co, 1999, 82, 66–94. Lisa Odham Stokes, *Historical Dictionary of Hong Kong Cinema*. Lanham, MD: Scarecrow Press, 2007, 223–24. Hall's book is exemplary for its detailed examination of Woo's stylistic signatures.

3   Leland Ryken, *The Apocalyptic Vision in Paradise Lost*. Ithaca, New York: Cornell University Press, 1970, 2. See also John T. Shawcross, "Confusion: The Apocalypse, the Millennium." *Milton and the Ends of Time*. Ed. Juliet Cummins. New York: Cambridge University Press, 2003, 106. I wish to thank Dr. Ryan Netzley for introducing me to this material.

4   Ryken, 3.

5   For various definitions of twentieth-century crisis cinema and the relationship to Hong Kong cinema see the various essays contained in *Crisis Cinema: The Apocalyptic Idea in Postmodern Narrative Film*. Ed. Christopher Sharrett. Washington, D.C.: Maisonneuve Press, 1993; Tony Williams, "Space, Place and Spectacle: The Crisis Cinema of John Woo." *The Cinema of Hong Kong: History, Arts, Identity*. Eds. Poshek Fu and David Desser. New York: Cambridge University Press, 2000, 137–57.

6   See Walter Schmithals, *The Apocalyptic Movement: Introduction and Interpretation*. Trans. John E. Steely. Nashville: University of Tennessee Press, 1975, 22–23; Juliet Cummins, "Matter and Apocalyptic Transformations in *Paradise Lost.*" *Milton and the Ends of Time*, 169.

7   Ken Simpson, "The Apocalypse in *Paradise Regained.*" *Milton and the Ends of Time*, 204.

8   See the postmodernist, a-historical, and non-materialistic reading of *A Better Tomorrow* in Karen Fang, *A Better Tomorrow*. Hong Kong: Hong Kong University Press, 2004. For other disturbing postmodernist approaches attempting to deny the implications of 1997, see Michael Walsh's review of *The Cinema of Hong Kong*. http://www.screeningthepast.com 15 (2003) and Karen Fang, "The Poverty of Sociological Studies of Hong Kong: Stokes and Hoover's *City on Fire.*" *http://film-philosophy.com/vol7-2003/n36fang.com*. For a response see Lisa Odham Stokes and Michael Hoover, "Comments on Karen Fang's Review of City on Fire: Hong Kong Cinema." http://film-philosophy.com/vol17-2003/n37stokeshoover.com. Abundant material exists concerning colony fears over 1997 in the light of Tiananmen Square. For Woo's own position at the time see Berenice Reynaud, "Woo in Interview." Translated by Terence Chang, *Sight and Sound*

3.5 (1993): 25. "I also wanted to use Vietnam as a mirror for what's going to happen in Hong Kong in 1997." This statement explicitly contradicts Woo's statement in the email interview Fang conducted on January 2003. See Fang, 119–20. Unlike Fang, Reynaud conducted a personal interview with John Woo. For another insightful recognition of the "1997" syndrome in relation to contemporary Hong Kong films and *Bullet in the Head* see David Bordwell, *Planet Hong Kong: Popular Cinema and the Art of Entertainment.* Cambridge, Mass.: Harvard University Press, 2000, 39–40, 109–10. Yau Ching remarks that very few Hong Kong films seek to confront political issues and even when the colony was full of anxiety concerning the implications of the 1984 Sino-British Declaration, several Hong Kong films such as *Hong Kong 1941* (1984), *Love in a Fallen City* (1984), *The Boat People* (1982), *Shanghai Blues* (1984), and *Homecoming* (1984) remained at the level of allegory by employing different times and places to depict the contemporary situation of Hong Kong by means of indirect allegory. See Yau Ching, *Filming Margins, Tang Shu Shuen: A Forgotten Hong Kong Woman Director.* Hong Kong: Hong Kong University Press, 2004, 95. According to Gina Marchetti, "If anything, after 1997, allusions to the relationship between Hong Kong and the PRC in the cinema have become even more pronounced." See her *Andrew Lau and Alan Mak's Infernal Affairs: The Trilogy.* Hong Kong University Press, 2007, 66. Marchetti makes further illuminating comments on Hong Kong cinema's mode of allegorical configuration on 68, 73, and 100. Such ideas are very relevant to the appropriate understanding of *Bullet in the Head.* For the importance of understanding contemporary cultural and historical factors concerning interpretation see also David Bordwell, *Making Meaning: Inference and Rhetoric in the Interpretation of Cinema.* Cambridge, Mass.: Harvard University Press, 1989, 265, 267; Janet Staiger, *Interpreting Films: Studies in the Historical Reception of American Cinema.* New Jersey: Princeton University Press, 1992.

9   David Loewenstein, "Afterword: 'The Time Is Come'." *Milton and the Ends of Time*, 241.

10   Martha P. Nochimson and Robert Cashill, "One Country: Two Visions: An Interview with Johnnie To." *Cineaste* 22.2 (2007): 36–39. See also

Stephen Teo, *Director in Action: The Films of Johnnie To*. London: British Film Institute, 2007.

11   This term is used by John Charles (40) but he does not employ it negatively. He uses it rather to describe a particular type of audience reaction that may not do justice to the film. As he continues, his use of the term becomes explicable in terms of the following sentence. "The film offers the same male bonding and high emotions that characterize Woo's earlier gangster pictures and unfolds amidst a surfeit of bloody but stylish violence. However, the superb melancholy score by James Wong and Romeo Diaz manipulates one's emotions to a greater degree, and the juxtaposition of physical cruelty, mental anguish, and human debasement in the face of war gives this film a more powerful impact. " For further observations on Woo's serious depiction of traumatic violence in the film, especially those scenes depicting Frank's debasement by violence in the Viet Cong camp, see James Steintrager, "*Bullet in the Head*: Trauma, Identity and Violent Spectacle." *Chinese Films in Focus: 25 New Takes*. Ed. Chris Berry. London: British Film Institute, 2003, 23–30. Hall, 137, also describes the film as "arguably a melodrama" and notes parallels to *Coriolanus*. *Titus Andronicus* could also be mentioned because of *Bullet in the Head*'s undeniably Gothic elements. The accusing silent nature of Frank's skull in the boardroom scene parallels Lavinia's mute presence when her father takes revenge on her violators. All these references demonstrate how multifaceted Woo's film is. It cannot really be defined by any one particular genre or influence.

12   See the "Tempting Fate" interview with Patrick Leung on the two-disc U.K. *Hong Kong Legends* DVD reissue of 2004.

13   "Life through a Lens," interview with John Woo. *Hong Kong Legends* DVD feature.

14   See Hall, 136. Darryl Pestilence, "John Woo (Ng Yu Sam)." http://victorian.fortunecity.com/durer/661/johnwoo

15   "Tempting Fate"; "Baptism of Fire: An Exclusive Interview with Jackie Cheung," Special Feature. *Hong Kong Legends*.

16   Stokes, 256; "Tempting Fate."

17   "Paradise Lost: An Interview with Waise Lee," "Reflections on *Bullet in the Head*." Special Features. *Hong Kong Legends*. Bey Logan audio-commentary.

18   Hall, 136.
19   Bey Logan audio-commentary; "Life through a Lens."

Chapter 2   Bullet in the Head

1   The actual Chinese names of the characters played by Tony Leung, Jackie Cheung, and Waise Lee are Ah-Bee, Ah-Fai, and Sai Wing respectively. Although the *Hong Kong Legends* DVD version retains these names, for the purpose of convenience I intend to use the Westernized versions that are familiar from most copies of the film currently in circulation today.
2   John Charles, *Hong Kong Filmography 1977–1997*. Jefferson, NC: McFarland & Co, 2000, 40.
3   The U.S. theatrical version of the film eliminated the graphic images of the three young stars oblivious of the fact that Woo wished to highlight the premature star status of these young actors. For the various narrative transformations "I'm a Believer" undergoes throughout the film see Kenneth E. Hall, *John Woo: The Films.* Jefferson, NC: McFarland & Co, 1999, 146. His examination of *Bullet in the Head* is exemplary both in terms of detail and nuance. Hall, 135–47.
4   See Richard Dyer, "Entertainment and Utopia." *Movie* 24 (1977): 36–43.
5   The photo between Kennedy and Elvis shows a young Chinese with his hair styled in the same manner as Elvis. He is probably one of the many 1960s Cantonese pop stars who imitated American music.
6   I use this term deliberately to evoke the common ideological understanding of Hollywood as the provider of entertainment. See Richard Maltby, *Harmless Entertainment: Hollywood and the Ideology of Consensus.* Metuchen, NJ: The Scarecrow Press, 1983.
7   Ringo is given the Chinese name of "Brother Keung" in the *Hong Kong Legends* DVD. As Bey Logan remarks on his audio-commentary, it is uncertain whether the English translation refers to Ringo Lam or Ringo Starr of the Beatles.
8   For Woo's knowledge of both Hawks and *Rio Bravo* see Hall, 7, 11, 39, 65, 158.

9   Woo's cameo role as a policeman may be the result of stepping in
      at the last moment for an actor who did not appear on the set. But
      it also represents the director's brief Hong Kong cinematic versions
      of a Hitchcock cameo where the author often appears during significant
      moments in his films. Despite the different images of the Hong Kong
      police force in cinema and reality, Woo presents himself firmly on
      the side of law and order as he does in his Taiwan police chief role
      in *A Better Tomorrow*. There he sincerely hopes for the redemption
      of Ti Lung's character throughout the film and approves the noble
      gesture he makes in the final scene by making his brother accept
      the validity of the law. By contrast, in Lung Gong's *Story of a
      Discharged Prisoner* (1967), Woo's character is a detective (played
      by the director himself) who constantly hounds Patrick Tse Yin's title
      character into becoming a police informant. Although this film
      influenced Woo in many ways, the differences are also significant.
      Unlike Lung Gong's other cameo appearance in *Teddy Girls* (1969),
      where he plays the negative role of Josephine Siao's stepfather, Woo
      always identifies himself with positive elements as seen in own cameo
      roles as in *Hand of Death* (1976) and *Hard Boiled* (1992) where
      Woo's barman character articulates moral values very close to the
      director. In his *Bullet in the Head* cameo, Woo probably wishes to
      state his disapproval of Ben's killing of Ringo. The director also made
      a rare acting appearance in Tony Leung Siu-hung's *Rebel from China*
      (1990) where he played a morally conscientious role of older brother
      to the main character.
10   See Stephen Heath, "Film and System: Terms of Analysis, Part I."
      Screen 16.1 (1975): 7–77.
11   The 1967 riots made an indelible impression on Hong Kong society
      and references to that incident occur in films as diverse as Anthony
      Chan Yau's *A Fishy Story* (1989), Evans Chan Yiu-shing's *Adeus
      Macao* (1999), and Wong Kar-wai's *2046* (2004). *A Fishy Story* opens
      with a montage sequence of historical stills, one of which shows a
      bomb disposal officer in full gear that obviously inspired the sequence
      in Woo's film. According to George Shen, "1967 saw many homemade
      grenades going off in Hong Kong and, for a time, the lefties ran wide
      (*sic*) in the city." He mentions that the left-wing film company Eng

Wah sent a camera crew to capture riot scenes intended to be used as background material for a Lung Kong film, *The Plague*, whose title was deliberately based on Albert Camus's play. During its production in 1968, left-wing activists accused the director of "inciting" the public with an *apocalyptic* vision of Hong Kong" (italics, mine). The film remained in limbo for two years until the distribution company re-edited the footage and removed some "blasting scenes." It was finally released in 1970 under the new title *Yesterday, Today, and Tomorrow*. See George Shen, "Filmdom Anecdotes." *Monographs of Hong Kong Veterans (2): An Age of Idealism: Great Wall and Feng Huang Days*. Ed. Wong Ain-ling. Hong Kong: Hong Kong Film Archive, 2001, 310. The Hong Kong Film Archive is performing a valuable service by filling in the gaps of Hong Kong cinema with these publications. *Yesterday, Today, and Tomorrow* is difficult to see and more work needs to be done on Lung Kung's influence on John Woo. Unfortunately, the film is not mentioned in the most recent oral history publication by the Hong Kong Film Archive but, hopefully, this may be rectified in the future. See "Oral History: Patrick Lung Kong." *The Glorious Modernity of Kong Ngee*. Ed. Wong Ain-ling. Hong Kong: Hong Kong Film Archive, 2006, 198–209. This film represented a type of social cinema generally regarded as taboo in the industry and Tsui Hark's scandalous *Dangerous Encounter: First Kind* (1980) may represent a later example of this trend. For a personal perspective concerning the significance of these riots see also Yau Ching, *Filming Margins, Tang Shu Shuen: A Forgotten Hong Kong Woman Director*. Hong Kong: Hong Kong University Press, 2004, 113–14.

12   Lisa Odham Stokes, *Historical Dictionary of Hong Kong Cinema*. Lanham, MD: Scarecrow Press, 2007, 422.

13   See *Vietnam War Films. Over 600 Feature, Made-for-TV, Pilot and Short Movies, 1939-1992, From The United States, Vietnam, France, Belgium, Australia, Hong Kong, South Africa, Great Britain and Other Countries*. Ed. Jean-Jacques Malo and Tony Williams. Jefferson, NC: McFarland & Co, Ltd., 1994. *Jump into Hell* was not available for viewing during the period this book was compiled.

14   "Tempting Fate," Special Feature. *Hong Kong Legends* DVD edition. According to James H., Chow Yun-fat was originally scheduled to play

Luke since he was impressed by the screenplay. But when Woo informed him of the character's secondary (but essential) role in the narrative, he did not want it to affect his contemporary star status he had sought since leaving television. See James H., "Bullet in the Head." http://www.cityonfire.com/hkfilms/ab/bulletinthe head.html.

15   Coincidentally enough according to Lisa Stokes (2007: 215), Philip Kwok's first screen appearance was in Zhang Che's *Marco Polo*.

16   These scenes (and others) may be found in the Fortune Star/Joy Films two-disc DVD edition of *Bullet in the Head* (2004). Were they also removed because of distributor fears about Woo "*inciting* the public with an *apocalyptic* vision of Hong Kong" as Lung Kong supposedly did in 1968? According to a June 17, 2002 interview with John Woo, the edited footage is now lost permanently since the studio laboratory threw them away, making any definitive "director's cut" impossible. See Jeffrey M. Anderson, Interview with John Woo: "Shooting the Breeze." http://www.combustiblecelluloid.com/interviews/johnwoo.shtml

17   Kevin Heffernan, "Do You Measure Your Friendship in Gold? The Genre Cinema of John Woo." A paper presented at the Hong Kong Cinema: Critical Perspectives Panel at the February 13, 1993 Meeting of the Society for Cinema Studies. I again wish to express my thanks to Kevin for allowing me access to this paper and a longer version written on May 6, 1992.

18   The urine sequence was probably removed for reasons of censorship and good taste but its excision leaves a glaring gap in other edited versions where Leong's hair is inexplicably wet before he is dragged away. According to Bey Logan's audio-commentary, it is based on an actual incident that happened to Ringo Lam who then told it to John Woo and Chow Yun-fat, the latter using it as a reference in *A Better Tomorrow*.

19   As Hall, 217, notes, "Paul's character owes more than a little to Fred C. Dobbs, Bogart's gold-corrupted prospector in *The Treasure of Sierra Madre* (John Huston, 1948)." Bey Logan also sees a reference to the final scene of Huston's *The Man Who Would Be King* (1975) in the later boardroom confrontation involving a skull but I would suggest that Sam Peckinpah's *Bring Me the Head of Alfredo Garcia* (1974) is a more likely source.

20 For a Marxist-psychoanalytic reading of both *Dracula* and
    Frankenstein in social and economic terms see Franco Moretti,
    "Dialectic of Fear." *Signs Taken for Wonders: Essays in the Sociology
    of Literary Forms*. Trans. Susan Fischer, David Forgacs, and David
    Miller. London: Verso, 1983, 83–108.

21 For Woo's debt to Peckinpah and how he reworks this particular
    influence see Hall, 3–7, 11, 66, and especially, 209, n.6, where he cites
    two important film industry authorities who recognize the differences
    between both directors.

22 Although critics such as Stephen Prince see Woo as one of the people
    responsible for the cult of excessive violence in contemporary
    Hollywood cinema, I believe this view is mistaken and that a detailed
    analysis of the director's films contradicts it. This is the reason for my
    chosen methodology of close textual analysis since close attention to
    detail is very important towards understanding the real significance
    of Woo's films. See Stephen Prince, *Savage Cinema: Sam Peckinpah
    and the Rise of Ultraviolent Movies*. Austin: The University of Texas
    Press, 1998, 168, 230, 231.

23 The current theatrical, VHS, and DVD versions of the film present
    this passage in silence while the earlier VHS Mandarin dialogue version
    had Sally's "Windflowers" song poignantly accompanying the quiet
    musings on the part of the three men who mourn her loss. This is one
    of the instances when the original sound mixture should have been
    retained since it forms an appropriate Eisenstein vertical montage
    complement to the scenes where sound, music, and image
    appropriately combine to depict a sad emotional moment in the
    film.

24 See James Steintrager, "*Bullet in the Head*: Trauma, Identity and
    Violent Spectacle." *Chinese Films in Focus: 25 New Takes*. Ed. Chris
    Berry. London: British Film Institute, 2003, 26–28. Jackie Cheung
    also regards his performance in *Bullet in the Head* as his best role to
    date. See "Baptism of Fire: An Exclusive Interview with Jackie Cheung,"
    Special Features. *Hong Kong Legends* two-disc edition of *Bullet in
    the Head*.

25 For Kubrick's influence on Woo see Hall, 11, 43–44, 63, 114–15, 118–
    19, 123, 132–39.

26   According to Bey Logan's audio-commentary, the presence of this child may evoke another well-known Vietnam War image, namely the photograph of a naked Vietnamese girl fleeing in terror along a road after being napalmed by American bombers.

27   See Stephen Teo, *A Touch of Zen*. Hong Kong: Hong Kong University Press, 2007, 22–25, for the significance of this imagery. By contrast, I believe Woo stresses the liberating powers of the day in this sequence rather than the nightly realm of the spider since the scenes showing Ben's slow recuperation occur during daylight.

28   I am thinking primarily of the key sequence in *Notorious* and the safe robbery scene in *Marnie*. Many other examples could be supplied.

29   Charles, 40. By contrast, Logan believes that the film should have ended with Ben's return to Jane since he thinks that the remaining ten minutes is detrimental to the film. The boardroom climax circulated on VCD versions of the film (which also lacked several other sequences) has been since restored on the two recent DVD reissues as a special feature. However, the boardroom ending may have resulted from producer demands to shorten the film rather than having anything to do with Woo's original intention. Even if Woo originally meant the film to end there, he could also have had second thoughts about it.

30   The reference to the 1991 Triad film about Limpy Ho, *To Be Number One* also featuring Waise Lee, is not accidental. Anybody familiar with Triad movies would immediately recognize that Paul is not involved in any legitimate business. See Tony Williams, "The Hong Kong Gangster Movie." *Gangster Film Reader*. Ed. Alain Silver and James Ursini. New York: Limelight Editions, 2007, 357–80.

31   See Martin Booth, *The Dragon Syndicates: The Global Phenomenon of the Triads*. New York: Carrol & Graf, 1999.

32   According to Waise Lee, he meant the death of Paul to contain overtones of a soul finally gaining release from torment. See "An Interview with Waise Lee," Special Features. Fortune Star/Joy Films DVD version of *Bullet in the Head*.

Chapter 3   Aftermath

1   See http://en.wikipedia.org/wiki/Bullet_in_the_Head.
2   These trailers are available as Special Features on the Fortune Star/ Joy Films DVD edition of *Bullet in the Head*.
3   See Stephen Teo, *Hong Kong Cinema: The Extra Dimensions*. London: BFI Publishing, 1997, 178.
4   Teo, 179.
5   Ibid.
6   See Lisa Odham Stokes and Michael Hoover, *City on Fire: Hong Kong Cinema*. London: Verso, 1999, 184. Chang's comment also evokes the bemused reaction of Robert Aldrich's businessman father concerning the conflict between integrity and economic corruption facing Jack Palance's Charlie Castle in *The Big Knife* (1955): "If a guy has to take or not to take $5,000 a week, what the hell is the problem?" See Charles Higham and Joel Greenberg, *The Celluloid Muse: Hollywood Directors Speak*. London: Angus and Robertson, 1969, 30.
7   Teo, 179–80.
8   See *Vietnam War Films*. Eds. Jean-Jacques Malo and Tony Williams.
9   See Stokes and Hoover, 167–200.
10   "Biting the Bullet: An interview with Simon Yam" and "Tempting Fire: An interview with Patrick Leung," Special Features. *Hong Kong Legends* DVD version.
11   "Baptism of Fire: An Interview with Jackie Cheung"; Bey Logan audio-commentary, Special Features. *Hong Kong Legends* DVD version.
12   Leung, "Tempting Fire."
13   Ibid. I also wish to thank Ken Hall who has supplied me with information from interviews with Terence Chang concerning the disputed nature of the original ending. Apparently, the film was meant to end with a fade to black after the boardroom sequence. Everyone was working frantically in shifts to try to develop a workable cut for general release since this was scheduled soon after the prescreening. Due to hostile responses on the part of distributors, demands were made for re-editing due to the length of the original prescreening version. Ken Hall, emails May 13, 2007. Woo may have had to shoot some new sequences such as Ben killing Paul in the boardroom and

the final ten minutes that occur in most versions today. Had Woo's original ended with no violent confrontation in the boardroom with Ben merely content to make Paul "lose face" in front of his Triad organization making his future existence a "living hell," similar to Frank's in the later Saigon scenes, then the film would have concluded on a more somber note like the Hong Kong theatrical version of *Infernal Affairs* where Andy Lau Tak-wah's character survives but remains trapped by his guilty conscience. If this is so, then Woo's envisaged ending paralleled the original climax of *Apocalypse Now* that provided no definitive resolution. It left Willard's decision to leave or take Kurtz's place entirely up to the audience.

14   See Kenneth E. Hall, *John Woo: The Films.* Jefferson, NC: McFarland & Co, 1999, 142. The Wikipedia entry on *Bullet in the Head* refers to two such sequences that probably represent what remains of the lost footage. In the first scene, Ben walks through some numbered footprints taped to the dance floor to demonstrate one of his dance moves. A fragment restored to the Fortune Star/Joy Films DVD version reveals a brief mid-shot of Ben instructing a student before clutching his chest in pain — a telling reference to his other role of leading his friends in that other dance of violence depicted in the credit sequence.

15   *The Beguiled* actually had a brief release in London but was hastily withdrawn from circulation and then safely released in England after the success of *Dirty Harry* over a year later.

16   Following Chow Yun-fat's withdrawal from the Mainland Chinese production *Red Cliff* (based on *The Romance of the Three Kingdoms*), Tony Leung returned to work with Woo for the first time since *Hard Boiled.*

17   For some alternative arguments concerning some of Woo's Hollywood films and their reception, see Tony Williams, "Woo's Most Dangerous Game: *Hard Target* and Neoconservative Violence." *Mythologies of Violence in Postmodern Media.* Ed. Christopher Sharrett. Detroit, Michigan: Wayne State University Press, 1999, 397–412; "*Face/Off:* Cultural and Institutional Violence within the American Dream." *Quarterly Review of Film and* Video 18.1 (2001): 31–38; "*Mission Impossible 2* or 'Alice in Cruiseland'." *Asian Cinema* 15.1 (2004): 203–16; Lisa Odham Stokes, "John Woo's War: Real (Reel) Dreams,

Windtalkers and the Hollywood Machine." *Asian Cinema* 15.1 (2004): 187–202. Alan Mak has also noticed how difficult it is for John Woo to "make a movie in Hollywood in his own style" with the exception of *Face/Off.* See Gina Marchetti , "Interview with Andrew Lau and Alan Mak." In *Andrew Lau and Alan Mak's Infernal Affairs: The Trilogy.* Hong Kong: Hong Kong University Press, 2007, 177.

Credits

Bullet in the Head (1990)

Producer-Director
John Woo Yu-sen

Cinematographers
Ardy Lam Kwok-wah
Wilson Chan Pui-kai
Somchai Kittikun
Horace Wong Wing-heng

Screenplay
John Woo
Patrick Leung Pak-kin
Janet Chun Siu-chun

Art Director
James Leung Wah-sang

Music
James Wong Jim
Romeo Diaz

Action Director
Lau Chi Ho

Cast
Tony Leung Chiu-wai (Ben)
Jack Cheung Hok-yau (Frank)
Waisie Lee, Chi-hung (Paul)
Yolinda Yan Cho-sin (Sally)
Simon Yam Tat-wah (Luke)
Fennie Yuen Kit-Ying (Jane)
Lam Cheung (Y. S. Leong)
Yee Tin-hung (Ringo)
John Woo (policeman)

Filmography

John Woo Yu-sen

Young Dragons (1973)
The Dragon Tamers (1974)
Hand of Death (1976)
Princess Chang Ping (1976)
Follow the Star (1977)
Money Crazy (1977)
Last Hurrah for Chivalry (1978)
Hello, Late Homecomers (1978)
From Riches to Rags (1979)
Laughing Times (1981)
To Hell with the Devil (1982)
Plain Jane to the Rescue (1982)
Run Tiger Run (1986)
The Time You Need a Friend (1986)
Heroes Shed No Tears (1986)
A Better Tomorrow (1986)
A Better Tomorrow 2 (1987)
The Killer (1989)

Just Heroes (1989)
Bullet in the Head (1990)
Once A Thief (1991)
Hard Boiled (1992)
Hard Target (1993)
Broken Arrow (1996)
Face Off (1997)
Mission Impossible 2 (2000)
Windtalkers (2002)
Paycheck (2003)
Red Cliff (2008)